W9-ADV-968

THE QUESTION OF HOW

Recent Titles in
Contributions in Women's Studies

American Women in Poverty
Paul E. Zopf, Jr.

Women Working: Comparative Perspectives in Developing Areas
Alma T. Junsay and Tim B. Heaton

Man Cannot Speak for Her. Volume I: A Critical Study of Early
Feminist Rhetoric
Karlyn Kohrs Campbell

Man Cannot Speak for Her. Volume II: Key Texts of the Early Feminists
Karlyn Kohrs Campbell

Gender, Bureaucracy, and Democracy: Careers and Equal Opportunity in
the Public Sector
Mary M. Hale and Rita Mae Kelly, editors

The President's Partner: The First Lady in the Twentieth Century
Myra G. Gutin

Women War Correspondents of World War II
Lilya Wagner

Feminism and Black Activism in Contemporary America: An
Ideological Assessment
Irvin D. Solomon

Scandinavian Women Writers: An Anthology from the 1880s to the 1980s
Ingrid Claréus, editor

To Bind Up the Wounds: Catholic Sister Nurses in the U.S. Civil War
Sister Mary Denis Maher

Women's Life Cycle and Economic Insecurity: Problems and Proposals
Martha N. Ozawa, editor

The Question of How

WOMEN WRITERS AND NEW PORTUGUESE LITERATURE

Darlene J. Sadlier

CONTRIBUTIONS IN WOMEN'S STUDIES,
NUMBER 109

GREENWOOD PRESS
New York • Westport, Connecticut • London

PQ
9033
.S24
1989

Library of Congress Cataloging-in-Publication Data

Sadlier, Darlene J. (Darlene Joy)
  The question of how : women writers and new Portuguese literature /
Darlene J. Sadlier.
    p. cm. — (Contributions in women's studies, ISSN 0147-104X;
no. 109)
  Bibliography: p.
  Includes index.
  ISBN 0-313-26844-4 (lib. bdg. : alk. paper)
  1. Portuguese fiction—Women authors—History and criticism.
2. Portuguese fiction—20th century—History and criticism.
3. Feminism and literature—Portugal—History—20th century.
I. Title. II. Series.
PQ9033.S24   1989
869.3'42099287—dc20   89-11731

British Library Cataloguing in Publication Data is available.

Library of Congress Catalog Card Number: 89-11731
ISBN: 0-313-26844-4
ISSN: 0147-104X

First published in 1989

Greenwood Press, Inc.
88 Post Road West, Westport, Connecticut 06881

Printed in the United States of America

∞™

The paper used in this book complies with the
Permanent Paper Standard issued by the National
Information Standards Organization (Z39.48-1984).

10 9 8 7 6 5 4 3 2 1

For James Otis Naremore

The book is the *written record* of a much broader, common, lived experience of creating a sisterhood through conflict, shared fun and sorrow, complicity and competition—an interplay not only of modes of writing but of modes of being, some of them conscious and some far less so, all of them shifting in the process, and all . . . still facing, even today, the question of *how*.

Authors' Afterword, *The Three Marias: New Portuguese Letters*

CONTENTS

Acknowledgments   ix

Introduction   xiii

I.   Radical Form in *Novas Cartas Portuguesas*   1

II. Modernism and Feminism in Fernanda Botelho's
     Xerazade e os Outros   25

III. Revolution and Representation in Lídia Jorge's
     O Dia dos Prodígios   49

IV. Sexuality and Repression in Hélia Correia's *Montedemo*   75

V.   The Language of Silence in Teolinda Gersão's
     O Silêncio   93

     Appendix. Feminism in Portugal: A Brief History   113

     Bibliography   131

     Index   135

ACKNOWLEDGMENTS

I was fortunate to receive research grants from the National Endowment for the Humanities, the Fulbright Commission, and the West European Center and the Office for Research and Graduate Development at Indiana University to assist me in the writing of this book.

Many individuals helped me while I was in Lisbon doing research. I would like to thank the women at the Comissão da Condição Feminina and, in particular, Bertina Sousa Gomes and Ivone Leal for arranging interviews with writers and representatives from women's organizations and for taking time out of their own busy schedules to discuss the commission's work in the area of women's rights. Also, the librarian, Maria Antónia Rosário, greatly facilitated my work in the archives housed in the offices of the commission.

I am indebted to Dennis Shaw, United States Cultural Attaché in Portugal, for having brought me into contact with the authors Lídia Jorge and Teolinda Gersão and for his gracious invitations to his home. I am also indebted to authors Maria Isabel Barreno, Fernanda Botelho, Natália Correia, Maria Teresa Horta, Lídia Jorge, Maria Regina Louro, and Teolinda Gersão; the physician and former political party leader Isabel do Carmo; Isabel Allegro of Graal; former Prime Minister Maria de Lourdes Pintasilgo; Fernanda Oliveira of the

Ministério de Educação; the women of the Movimento Democrático de Mulheres; and the staff of the magazine *Mulheres*—all of whom were more than generous in taking time to discuss with me literary, social, political, and other matters that touch the lives of women in Portugal. I also want to express a special word of thanks to Maria Augusta de Figueiredo and her family for opening their home to me in the summer of 1987.

In addition to Professors Doris J. Turner and Fred Clark, with whom I have discussed my work over the last few years, I wish to acknowledge my colleague Heitor Martins, who first called my attention to the writer Fernanda Botelho and her novel *Xerazade e os Outros*. It is not for this alone that I thank him. He has been more than generous with his time—reading over drafts of my chapters, helping with translations, and giving me the benefit of his friendship and intelligence. Finally, throughout the research and writing of the book, I received invaluable advice and support from my husband, James Naremore, who spent many hours of his own precious research time reading and commenting on the manuscript. Suffice it to say that without his help and constant encouragement this book might never have been written.

Bantam, Doubleday, Dell Publishing Group, Inc. Reprinted by permission of Doubleday and Victor Gollancz.

Xerazade e os Outros by Fernanda Botelho. Copyright 1964 by Livraria Bertrand. Reprinted with permission of author and Livraria Bertrand, Lisbon, Portugal.

INTRODUCTION

Since its revolution in 1974, Portugal has produced a large number of writings by and about women. Names such as Lídia Jorge, Teolinda Gersão, Hélia Correia, Clara Pinto Correia, Maria Gabriela Llansol, Olga Gonçalves, Maria Regina Louro, Luísa Costa Gomes, and Margarida Carpinteiro have become prominent in the nation's literary circles, and some of them are known internationally. In addition to these newer writers, several women of the prerevolutionary period, including Agustina Bessa-Luís, Maria Isabel Barreno, Fernanda Botelho, Maria Teresa Horta, Maria Velho da Costa, and Natália Correia, continue to publish and are widely read. The publishing firms O Jornal, Ulmeiro, Dom Quixote, Relógio d'Água, and in particular Editora Rolim have done much to promote works by women; in fact today, for the first time in history, there are at least as many women as men publishing books in Portugal.

This book attempts to acknowledge some of these developments through a close analysis of five texts by contemporary women writers. Although I describe the texts in detail, I have tried to avoid a simple series of "readings." One of my purposes is to introduce an important and unified body of literature to a broader reading audience, in the belief that this literature represents a major contribution to European culture. At the same time, I want to deal with questions of ideology and narrative that are relevant to Western literature as a whole. Contemporary Portugal offers an especially fascinating conjuncture of social revolution, literary experiment, and feminist practice; its women writers have repeatedly dealt with the most difficult issues in the sphere of cultural politics, and I believe we can understand the full implication of their work only by paying close attention to the ideology of form. Hence, I have not designed the book as an encyclopedic overview or a general introduction. Instead, I concentrate on exemplary works, treating them as microcosms and foregrounding their artistic strategies.

Throughout, I have tried to place the writers selected in the political and social background that has determined their practice. Perhaps the most important feature of this background is that, for nearly fifty years, until 1974, Portugal was ruled by a fascist regime. These women all grew up during the Salazar dictatorship, and in one form or another they directly experienced its policies. Interestingly, however, very few of them write about politics in a direct fashion. Generally speaking, they concentrate on more subtle forms of social control that affect the country as a whole and women in particular. Inevitably, they are deeply concerned with the politics of representation, and in different ways they attempt to devise a form that will be adequate to materials that older literature repressed, ignored, or distorted. In a sense, it could be said that they are all Virginia Woolf's sisters, even if they write in ways quite different from Woolf, and even if they have not been directly influenced by her.

To give a more extended sense of the social context within which these women write, I have added an appendix, which provides a brief historical account of the status of women in Portugal and mentions some of the writers and political activists who helped to create modern Portuguese culture. My discussion of feminist history serves as a kind of sociological afterword, pointing to the way in which women's lives have always been determined in the last instance by a patriarchal state. Because the historical material has an indirect relation to the book proper, it is placed slightly apart; nevertheless, some readers may want to glance at the appendix first before going on to the literary analysis. The appendix contains useful information that has never before been discussed in English, and it helps to establish certain crucial facts about Portuguese reality. Clearly, the writers discussed here are working in response to hundreds of years of oppression, and their stories can be fully understood only if the reader appreciates the larger social and political narrative that helped shape them.

The substance of my work consists of an analysis of five books, arranged in a roughly chronological order. In each case I try to put the individual books in context, sometimes describing the writer's career and sometimes sketching in the social and historical milieu of the fiction. This method allows me to elucidate a series of rather unorthodox works, most of which are unknown to English-speaking readers, and to concentrate on details of style and form that are central to my discussion. To ensure a wider readership, I have (unless indicated otherwise) provided my own translations of the Portuguese. The purpose of these literal translations is to enable the non-Portuguese reader to follow the argument. I have not attempted more artful, "literary" renditions, hoping to convey the style of the writers by quoting the original Portuguese alongside the English version. I should add that, in the case of Lídia Jorge, whose text is filled with terms and expressions particular to the Portuguese Algarve, the translations are merely approximations of a peculiar language that is at once demotic and baroque.

I selected these particular texts for several reasons. First, they seem to me unusually compelling and relevant works of fiction, marked by high intelligence and impressive literary skill. They also pose a series of difficult problems for readers and require thoughtful analysis. As a group, they represent an interesting variety of technical approaches— experiments in montage or polyphonic writing, in unusual forms of literary expressionism, and in a number of smaller scale representational devices that affect virtually every aspect of narrative. My repeated concern with such matters, however, is not merely technical. My first and last purpose is to investigate what Portuguese literary women have to say about their culture, but it soon becomes apparent that the best of the new women's "voices" are as much concerned with *how* to write as with what to say. In fact, although all of the writers speak a "woman's discourse," they do not concentrate exclusively on domesticity or the experience of women; Lídia Jorge, for example, often writes about the rural or marginal culture of the southern Algarve, showing how this culture is oppressed by militarism, industrial capitalism, and modern forms of state power. If there is any feature that they all have in common, it is less their overt content than their slightly alienated, problematic relationship with the literary forms they have inherited. It is not enough for these women to say different things; they must also speak differently.

It would be wrong to describe these writers as a school or a movement, since they have no manifesto, no special journal or publishing company, and no common program for literature. They are somewhat like what Marxist theory would call a *fraction*—a group of middle-class women who have political attitudes that are in some ways opposed to the dominant culture. The thing that most connects them, however, is not politics but an almost unconscious reaction against traditional realist narrative. In one way or another they all attempt to achieve literary estrangement, as if to demonstrate that the form of literature is itself ideological. What interests me most about their work is this fusion of modernist or postmodernist experiment with a social critique. For that reason I have omitted discussion of one writer who is arguably the most influential woman of letters in contemporary Portugal: Agustina Bessa-Luís, who since 1950 has written more than twenty novels, all of which have been widely read. However interesting Bessa-Luís might be, she tends to work from a conventional epistemology, and her books do not deal with the same order of problems as the texts I have chosen. In aesthetic terms, her writing is conservative, whereas the five texts discussed here are all radically transgressive, raising fundamental questions about literary as well as social politics.

These texts are theoretical in the best sense of the term, and as a group they form an unusually significant body of women's literature. Some of them are more progressive and liberating than others, but they are all worthy of our closest attention. Portugal may be a small country and a latecomer to democracy, but its women writers have produced remarkable works, capable of speaking to us all. To study these writers is not only to become acquainted with a series of important European novels, but also to learn more about the complex responses of women to modern society in general.

I

RADICAL FORM IN
NOVAS CARTAS PORTUGUESAS

*. . . call me Mary Beton, Mary Seton, Mary Carmichael or by any other name you
please—it is not a matter of any importance . . .*
Virginia Woolf, A Room of One's Own

My name is legion, for we are many.
Mark 5:9

Few works in the history of Portuguese letters have captured the widespread attention and critical acclaim generated by the 1972 publication of *Novas Cartas Portuguesas* by Maria Isabel Barreno, Maria
Teresa Horta, and Maria Velho da Costa. Banned by the Portuguese
right-wing government shortly after publication, it was finally released
in 1974 and, within a year, was translated into nearly every modern
European language. In January 1975, upon publication of Helen R.
Lane's English version, the book was discussed in major literary reviews throughout the United States. And yet, even though more than
a decade has passed since then, the significance of *Novas Cartas
Portuguesas* as a pioneer work by three women writers on women remains largely unexplored. The purpose of this chapter is to begin a
process of analysis, viewing the international best-seller within a

broader context of Portuguese reality and examining its importance as a sociopolitical document. But I shall also address a more theoretical issue related to the form of the book, an issue whose implications are of central import for women's literature.

To clarify these matters, it will be helpful to review the circumstances under which the book was produced. Although much of this information has been discussed elsewhere,[1] a brief summary of the most salient points will lay the groundwork for my discussion of form and ideology.

The significance of the events leading up to the publication of *Novas Cartas Portuguesas* by the "Three Marias," as they have become internationally known, can be fully appreciated only within the context of the economic and sociopolitical situation in Portugal during the turbulent years preceding the April 1974 revolution. Portugal had been under the thumb of António de Oliveira Salazar since 1928, when he was appointed minister of finance—historically speaking not a very powerful position in the political hierarchy, but one which Salazar made so through his astute understanding of Portugal's economy and his adept handling of funds, which resulted in his complete and uncontested control of the country's coffers. I will not attempt to outline here the years of Salazar's authoritarian rule. But it is important to understand that *Novas Cartas Portuguesas* is in every sense a political book, intended to attack the measures born out of Salazar's repressive government. These measures, enforced even after his death in 1970 by the Marcelo Caetano administration, directly and indirectly affected the rights and freedom of women in Portugal.

One particularly illuminating example of Salazar's attempt to restrict women's civil liberties can be found in a 1933 speech, delivered from the headquarters of the National Union, which is widely recognized as embodying the essence of his political beliefs. In this speech, Salazar gave considerable attention to the issue of labor and the family structure:

Women's work outside the family sphere disintegrates home life, separates its different members, and makes them strangers to each other. . . . Life in common disappears; the work of educating the children suffers and families become smaller. Through the unsatisfactory and difficult task of regulating the family budget, in the running of the home, and in the provision of food and clothing, a serious loss is exper-

ienced, and it is very rarely that it is actually made up by the wages received. (Salazar 1939, 162)

Salazar concluded his statement on women and the work force as follows:

> We consider that it is the man who should labor and maintain the fam-
> ily and we say that the work of the married woman outside her home,
> and, similarly that of the spinster who is a member of the family, should
> not be encouraged. There never was a good housekeeper who did not
> find plenty to do. (162)

Salazar not only attempted to confine women to the home, but he
also dictated the housekeeping role they were to assume. Some twenty
years later, his position with regard to women was as reactionary and
intransigent as ever. In an interview conducted at Salazar's home, the
French journalist and writer Christine Garnier asked the chief-of-
state if he could possibly check the liberation movement that was
gaining momentum among Portuguese women. His response was

> How could I break the wave of feminine independence which is coming
> over the world? Women show such a need for freedom, such a frenzy for
> the pleasures of life. They don't understand that happiness is reached
> through renunciation rather than enjoyment. . . . The great nations
> should set an example by confining women to their homes. But these
> great nations seem oblivious to the fact that the solid family structure
> cannot exist where the wife's activity is outside the home. And so the
> evil spreads and each day becomes more dangerous. What can I do, I
> myself, in Portugal? I know only too well, alas, that all my efforts to
> bring women back to older ways of living have remained practically use-
> less! (Quoted in Garnier 1954, 7)

Despite Salazar's claim of ineffectuality, he did in fact succeed in
passing a law prohibiting married women from gaining employment
as nurses or employees in the Ministry of Foreign Affairs. Later, he
attempted to broaden this law to cover all types of work but failed
because of objections raised by various groups, including the Catholic Church.

While many women did filter into the work force in Portugal in the
1940s and 1950s as teachers, journalists, and factory workers, the ma-

jority, true to Salazar's dictates, remained at home. Christine Garnier made note of this fact:

> ... they [the women] stay in the shadow of their homes with heads bowed before a husband. As I said this I thought of those young women I had seen, with their soft, sad eyes, catching their high heels on the irregular pavement of Lisbon, somewhat embarrassed to find themselves in streets belonging to men. As soon as the summer sun starts shining, they withdraw to the *quinta*, to their homes in the country. And the year over, they struggle to keep by their side husbands who prefer to talk with other men in the noisy cafés of the Rossio. (Garnier 1954, 6)

Even during the liberal 1960s, little happened to change the course of women's rights in Portugal. The suffrage movement had won women the right to vote in England in 1918 and in America in 1920, but it was not until 1969, one year after Salazar fell ill and Caetano took office, that voting privileges were extended to all women in Portugal. While this act appeared to be a progressive move by the government, it was promulgated only after the publication of a survey which reported that, on the whole, women were more conservative than men. In other words, women were more likely to use their vote to support the status quo (Gallagher 1983, 167, 189 n. 6).

By 1972, the time was ripe for a book which would make public the plight of women in Portugal as well as testify to the struggle of women worldwide. The idea for such a book was conceived by Maria Isabel Barreno shortly after the publication of Maria Teresa Horta's *Minha Senhora de Mim* (Milady of Me), a slim volume of fifty-nine poems which explores, through images of the female body, the themes of love and passion. Public response to this book was overwhelmingly critical because of Horta's use of certain taboo words and her highly explicit descriptions of physical love. The official response to the book was equally negative; within a matter of weeks, all copies in the bookstores had been confiscated and the book was banned for being erotic. At this point, Barreno decided that, if a book written by a woman "who wrote freely like a man" could provoke such a reaction, it was time three or four women together wrote about the problems women faced in Portugal.

At this time, Horta and Barreno were already established in the literary arena. Horta was perhaps the more widely known for her poems, which she began publishing in 1960. By the time her controversial *Minha Senhora de Mim* appeared in print, she had already written eight books of poetry and the stories *Ambas as Mãos sobre o Corpo* (Both Hands over Her Body). Barreno's career began in 1968 with the publication of the novel *De Noite as Árvores São Negras* (At Night the Trees Are Black) followed two years later by another novel entitled *Os Outros Legítimos Superiores* (The Other Legitimate Superior Ones). Maria Velho da Costa was less well known, although she had published a volume of short stories and the novel *Maina Mendes*. All three women were in their early thirties, had been educated in convent schools, were married, and had sons. They all worked outside the home: Horta wrote for a Lisbon-based newspaper, and Barreno and Velho da Costa, who were childhood friends, worked together as researchers in the Ministry of Economics.

Barreno proposed to the other two a collaborative project, the purpose of which would be to examine their similar problems and concerns as women and radical writers in Portugal. After some hesitation by Horta, who was concerned whether she could write effectively as part of a group, they agreed to meet twice a week: once for lunch in a public restaurant, to discuss topics such as their childhood experiences and their experiences as young women, working women, wives, and mothers; and once in the evening in private, to talk over what each had written during the week. Each was required to exchange letters regularly with the other two, and those letters as well as other writings would form the corpus of the book. No rules were imposed with regard to the genre, style, or content of what they wrote so that their material would reflect freely their day-to-day experiences as well as the conditions under which they worked. All the material would be dated but would not bear a signature.

After a few weeks of exchanging letters, the women decided to use the seventeenth-century classic *Lettres Portugaises* as the central motif around which all the other material would revolve. While the authenticity of these letters has long been debated (it is generally agreed that they were written by the Frenchman, Guilleragues, who published them in Paris in 1669), they were originally attributed to a young Portuguese nun, Mariana Alcoforado, who supposedly wrote them to her lover, Noël Bouton, a Frenchman who had come to Portugal to help liberate the country from Spanish rule. Sent to a convent at an early age, Mariana ultimately became a nun, like many other women who had no alternative to the cloister. When she was twenty-five, she met Bouton and fell in love. Fearful of the consequences of their affair, Bouton, without a word, left Portugal for France. Between 1667 and 1668, Mariana supposedly wrote five letters to Bouton which reveal the fears, the moments of faith, and the subsequent doubts and despair of a woman abandoned by the man she loves. Bouton later became the chevalier of Chamilly and marshal of France. Mariana never saw him again.

Whether or not these letters or ones like them were in fact written by Mariana Alcoforado is unimportant. For the three contemporary women writers, the letters became symbolic of the plight of all women who are confined, whether by an actual convent or by a reactionary political system. They took up the story of Mariana, elaborated on it, and created new letters from Mariana to her lover, friends, and family. In addition to these new letters by Mariana, they composed their own letters, as well as poems, essays, word games, reports, entries from diaries—all of which exposed the suffering and separation experienced by women in Portugal as a result of repressive social and economic measures, emigration, colonialism, conscription, and the wars in Africa.

In 1972, the authors of *Novas Cartas Portuguesas* saw their collaborative work displayed in bookstores throughout the country, even though Portuguese law clearly stated that anyone working on a book judged censorable after publication could be arrested and put on trial. In Natália Correia, a poet and novelist and then editor-in-chief of the publishing firm Estúdios Cor, *Novas Cartas Portuguesas* found a publisher willing to take a chance. Because of the strict laws regulating the content of materials, one typesetter refused to work on the book; others, in an effort to protect themselves from possible prosecution, denounced it to the authorities. In spite of all this, the work was printed, and all but about 100 copies of the estimated 3,000 printed were sold.

The arrest of the Three Marias took place in the spring of 1972. They were charged with, among other crimes, "abuse of the freedom of the press" and "outrage to public decency." The authorities made numerous attempts to uncover the author of certain highly erotic pages which were the main object of dispute. The women refused to identify the author of any section in the book. Anonymity had long been planned by the Three Marias in the face of strict censorship, so that no one of them could be singled out and prosecuted on the grounds of violating public morality. As a result of their silence, all three went to trial.

Court proceedings were initiated in 1973; however, the trial underwent numerous postponements and even a change of judge. Bail was set for all three women, and each suffered reprimands from her respective employer. Horta, denied her byline in the Lisbon newspaper for which she regularly wrote, was forced to publish articles anonymously; Barreno and Velho da Costa were informed that if found guilty they would lose their jobs at the ministry. The trial lasted from July 1973 to May 1974. On the first day, the courtroom was filled to capacity. The Portuguese public as well as foreign correspondents, book publishers, lawyers, and women's groups from around the world had come to witness what had already become an international incident. The judge quickly moved that the courtroom be cleared, his reason being that immoral and offensive terms would appear in the testimony. As the months passed, however, the tenor of the trial was affected by the changing political climate. The prosecutor, who seemed to sympathize with the defendants rather than press for their conviction, was dismissed, and another took his place. The women were to be sentenced in mid-April 1974, but the judge, aware of the rising tensions in the political arena, delayed sentencing for another three weeks. On April 25, the military seized control of the government. On May 7, the same judge who had presided over the proceedings announced that all charges against the three women had been dropped and that their case had been dismissed. He released their book and congratulated them for having written a work of the highest literary quality.

Despite the Lisbon judge's dictate, and despite the considerable journalistic attention that has been focused on the above events, to date relatively very little has been written about *Novas Cartas Portuguesas* as a work of literature. This is perhaps not surprising for, on the face of it, the book is difficult to describe with the standard critical terminology. Even the authors themselves refer to their book as a "thing," which suggests their inability, or perhaps better, their reluctance to categorize it. Inevitably, one's first impression of the book is of a hodgepodge—letters, essays, and poems, randomly assembled, whose only apparent unity is derived from the theme of women's liberation. After several readings, however, one can perceive more intriguing aspects of the form, so that the very structure of the book takes on political implications. In this sense, the book has a specifically literary interest. It is not only a challenge to orthodox ideas, but also a different kind of representation, an attempt to reshape the culture's "way of seeing."

We might say that the literary forms inherited by the Three Marias are a bit like those "irregular" paving stones in Lisbon described by Christine Garnier. Just as the stones were designed for men's shoes and not for high heels, so the traditional architecture of European literature was not shaped for women's experience of the world. Hence a great many of the major women writers of this century have been concerned with the problem of form. Virginia Woolf commented on this fact in A Room of One's Own, when she observed how unwieldy the classical tradition was when women tried to use it: "And I . . . ponder[ed] how a woman nowadays would write a poetic tragedy in 5 acts. Would she use verse?—would she not use prose rather?" (Woolf 1967, 116). Perhaps because of its relatively short history, the novel is the literary genre that women have found easiest to adapt to their ends. But Woolf raised a question that other women have also asked: "And who shall say that even now the 'novel' . . . this most pliable of all forms is rightly shaped for [a woman's] use? No doubt we will find her knocking that into shape for herself when she has the free use of her limbs; and providing some new vehicle, not necessarily in verse, for the poetry in her" (116). In other words, Woolf believed that women would ultimately reshape literature, seeking out a form of representation that is more "comfortable" for them.

Novas Cartas Portuguesas confirms what Woolf predicted. As women, and as radical writers in a society just emerging into democracy, the Three Marias wrote a book that subscribes to no particular genre and refuses the logic of traditional literary form. There are many reasons for this phenomenon, but one of the most obvious is the fact that the unusual conditions under which they wrote determined a condensed, elliptical type of book. Virginia Woolf had described a roughly similar situation when she addressed herself to the social and economic situation of women writers in England in the second decade of the twentieth century:

> The book has somehow to be adapted to the body, and at a venture one could say that women's books should be shorter, and more concentrated than those of men, and framed so that they do not need long

hours of steady and uninterrupted work. For interruptions there will always be. (116-17)

This crude, practical reality was in fact an issue for the Three Marias,
who, as working women, as well as wives and mothers, were unable to
spend long hours together. As we have seen, *Novas Cartas Portuguesas*
was born of twice weekly meetings at which they exchanged ideas and
correspondences; consequently, they wrote in disconnected fragments, and their individual letters, poems, and essays rarely exceed
three or four printed pages. In this sense, their work is shorter and
more concentrated, roughly analogous to what Woolf had assumed
working women would have to produce.

In another, more important sense, however, the form of *Novas
Cartas Portuguesas* was developed in relation to the conventions
which the authors inherited, and which they adapted to potentially
subversive ends. Chief among these inherited forms was the tradition
of epistolary narrative, which motivates not only the title of the book
but also its opening statement: "Pois que toda a literatura é uma longa
carta a um locutor invisível, presente, possível ou futura paixão que
liquidamos, alimentamos ou procuramos" (Barreno, Horta, and
Velho da Costa 1972, 9) (all of literature is a long letter to an invisible
other, a present, a possible, or a future passion that we rid ourselves of,
feed or seek) (Lane 1975, 151).[2] The term *cartas* in the title refers to
letters or epistles in the general sense but also to the original letters
purportedly written by the Portuguese nun, Mariana Alcoforado, in
the seventeenth century. In *Novas Cartas Portuguesas*, the Three
Marias are clearly alluding to a national literary classic and to a sort of
"mother" from whom they have learned a theme, but they also allude
to the epistolary novel in general—a form long associated with
women and writing.[3] The book's chief mode is therefore a series of letters which constitutes a roughly narrative order, even though it is not a
single, unitary narrative. The epistles consist of exchanges between
the authors, letters from fictional wives to husbands, "new" letters
from Mariana (addressed not only to Bouton but also to her family
and friends), letters from various fictional women to their lovers, and
letters from fictional mothers to daughters. In this way the book both
derives from and breaks with the novelistic tradition, opting for a radically fragmented form, a modernist montage of prose, poetry, excerpts
from diaries, sketches, essays, and other forms.

We can get a better sense of the book's radical nature if we separate out some of the kinds of writing and notice their functions. For example, poetry of diverse sorts—erotic lyrics, verse epistles, ballads, and *cantigas*—is scattered through the text. Although a close study of the individual poems is impossible here, it is important to note that nearly all the poetry violates the established Portuguese norms of literary taste. In a general sense, the poems are constructed out of a language of the body—a woman's language—which explores, from a female perspective, the relationship between men and women, between women and other women, and, perhaps most important, between women and their image of themselves. Everywhere the verse functions to express private, repressed sexual experience which had been displaced in the romanticized story of the original Mariana; it openly explores physical and erotic love, male and female anatomies, masturbation, orgasm, erection—topics which had long been acceptable to talk and write about from a male perspective, were judged censorable when articulated from a strictly female point of view. And if in some instances the poems violate the social norms by being graphic and erotic, in other instances they defy tradition by presenting new, positive images of women to replace those sustained by centuries of national verse. This second purpose is of course not restricted to the poems, but because of the reduced and concentrated nature of poetic language, some of its best achievements are seen in this form:

Eis-nos de luta
expostas
sem vencer os dias

as verilhas
certas
no passo retomado

o rever das casas e das causas
o revolver das coisas
que dormiam

Diária é a escolha
o movimento insano
o sossego manso e mais pesado
daquilo que desperta e não quebramos

daquilo que rasgamos
e dobramos
carta por carta em seu perfil exacto

Fêmeas somos
fiéis à nossa imagem
oposição sedenta que vestimos
mulheres pois sem procurar vantagem
mas certas bem dos homens que cobrimos

E jamais caça
seremos

ou objeto
dado

nem voluntário odor
de bosque seco

vidro dizemos
pedra
caminhada

em se chegar a nós
de barca
ou vento

Remota viração que se reparte
esta que usamos em cumprir
sustento

de pressuposta amarra
em que ficamos

apartadas dos outros
e tão perto (40–41)

      ★ ★ ★

Here we are
engaged in combat
our flanks exposed
the past
not yet overcome

our loins
self-assuredly
resume their stride

examining anew
our hearths and our hearts' reasons
rousing things
that were sleeping

The choice a daily one
our pace frantic
our repose restful
yet weighing more heavily upon us
than what is awakening
yet not breaking our spirit
than what we are tearing apart
and folding into a clean-cut shape
letter by letter

We are females
faithful to our image
thirsting opposition the raiment
in which we clothe ourselves
women not seeking the upper hand
yet very sure of the men we couple with

Firmly resolved
never to be a prey
or an object
abjectly surrendering

or deliberately giving off
the odor of dry wood

calling ourselves glass
stone
traveled across

as we journey toward ourselves
born by a barque
or by the wind

A far-ranging
shared circling round and round
this path we follow
to find sustenance
to sink firm foundations
for the dreamed-of anchorage

where we now remain
separated from others
and yet so close (49–51)

The book also contains essays and fictional sketches which serve as
a forum for less individualized, more sociological accounts of the female experience. Among the topics these forms address are incest,
rape, wife-beating, prostitution, economic dependency, and suicide;
as a result, the purely imaginative, narrative aspects of the book are
seen against a background of documented abuses and systemic conditions. In addition to the essays and sketches are other, less conventional modes of writing: a fictional medical-psychiatric report on the
condition of a woman named Mariana A., two fictional compositions
by schoolgirls on "duties" and "words," and various dramatic monologues by fictional characters. Furthermore, whenever it wishes, the
book mixes actual documentary evidence with this material, directly
quoting excerpts from a variety of other texts, including a statement
on adultery from the *Portuguese Penal Code* and portions of Collin de
Plancy's *Dictionary of Witchcraft*—a nineteenth-century work which
describes the case histories of women who, thought to be in league
with the devil, were exorcised, exiled, or condemned to death.

Perhaps even more than the poems, sketches, and essays, these lat-
ter modes emphasize the degree to which the Three Marias were willing to dispense with the ordinary romantic notions of "organic unity"
and to challenge the early distinctions between fiction and history.
The women also included a series of word games which "play" with the
letters of the names Mariana and Maria Ana, or which form a kind of
crossword puzzle, obsessively spelling out such traditional feminine
roles as "mother," "housekeeper," and "mistress." In this minor way,
the authors show an interesting tendency to break with one of the
most cherished conventions of bourgeois realism: somewhat like
European modernists of earlier generations (but for very different rea-

sons), they challenge the notion that language is transparent, and they make a rebellious political game of the signifier.

As the above description of its fragmented and multiform nature suggests, *Novas Cartas Portuguesas* cannot be called a novel in any sense of the word. Nevertheless it embodies certain narrative and temporal qualities generally associated with the novel, and it draws upon novelistic form to achieve a pattern of development. It is clearly based upon the epistolary formula first developed in the seventeenth-century *Lettres Portugaises* and later popularized by Samuel Richardson in the eighteenth century, even though it contains verse epistles, lyric poems, and essays, as well as other fictional and non-fictional forms. At its most basic level, it adopts the epistolary novel's central premise of two or more individuals striving to maintain their relationship through letters. Hence, although it rejects certain formal and conceptual notions underlying epistolary prose, *Novas Cartas Portuguesas* nevertheless embodies a kind of tension associated with the novel, a tension produced and sustained by individuals who seek to overcome the obstacles keeping them apart.[4] Its most decisive and interesting break with tradition is the way in which it rejects the romantic, sentimentalized story of star-crossed lovers destined for either marriage or death; instead it opts for a story about women who, separated from one another by society, strive toward unity through a process of self-awareness and self-understanding.

The various letters, poems, and other entries do not obey the temporal logic of realist narrative; for example, a "new" letter written by Mariana Alcoforado in the seventeenth century may be followed by a letter from a young woman to her boyfriend in the 1960s. Nonetheless a story is being told, and it unfolds through the thematic juxtaposition of individual entries which connect the similar problems of different women in different times. In this respect, it is important to note that each entry bears a date that corresponds to the day when it was actually written. The book begins with a letter dated March 1, 1971, and ends with a piece written on October 25, 1971. Hence, while we read back and forth in time, we are constantly made aware of another temporal dimension, a linear development which is at once separate from and part of the individual letters and poems. For, although the letters, poems, and essays represent a particular historical time which is nonlinear in progression, their placement in the text is determined by a chronology based on the dialogues between and the communications exchanged by the Three Marias.

The narrative element of *Novas Cartas Portuguesas* centers most prominently on the original story of Mariana Alcoforado, who rises above the tragedy of her love affair to denounce those who comply with and enforce a system that isolates and destroys women by keeping them behind walls. But this story cannot be understood without the reader's full knowledge of the plot in *Lettres Portugaises*. In other words, *Novas Cartas Portuguesas* relies upon a quite consciously intertextual device, deriving its narrative feel from something that has been developed elsewhere. Certain themes of the earlier book provide suggestions that the contemporary authors have elaborated and given a new development. The most obvious of these is Mariana's sense of separation and loss, stemming from her lover's hasty departure, which fills the pages of *Lettres Portugaises*. Mariana is a woman confined within the walls of a cloister who, in order to release some of her anguish, requests her brother's permission to write letters—the sole approved outlet for her. The process of writing itself therefore becomes a crucial issue in the original letters, for it is writing alone that enables her to voice her thoughts and opinions in an isolated world where silence prevails. This issue takes on a poignant and ironic dimension in the fifth and final letter in the original collection, when Mariana's rage and passion are somewhat quelled. She beseeches her lover not to write to her. Although she begins by stating it is her last communication to him, later in the letter she promises to write him once more if only to show him how composed she has become.

While the epistle was the means by which Mariana conveyed her love to Bouton in *Lettres Portugaises*, in the more radical *Novas Cartas Portuguesas*, the epistle itself becomes Mariana's primary focus of attention as a means toward self-understanding. This development can be seen in the "new" letter entitled "VI e última carta de D. Mariana Alcoforado, freira em Beija, ao cavaleiro de Chamilly, escrita no dia de Natal do ano da graça de mil seiscentos e setenta e um" (331) (Sixth and Final Letter from Dona Mariana Alcoforado, a Nun in Beja, to the Chevalier de Chamilly, Written on Christmas Day of the Year of Grace 1671 [342]), which, in tone and content, corresponds to the letter of which Mariana spoke in the final communication of the original collection. Of immediate import are the dates of this new correspondence. Ostensibly written by the nun in 1671 but bearing

the signed date of composition of 1971, it marks the historical significance of *Novas Cartas Portuguesas*: after 300 years of silence, it revives
and reexamines the story of Mariana, whose cloistered existence
stands as a symbol of the separated and powerless condition of
modern-day woman. Unlike the original Mariana, this nun is not
writing a letter with the intention of sending it to the chevalier; rather,
her interest is in the act of writing itself. "Não é meu fito dar-vos a ler
jamais estas linhas que outro não têm que o de serem escritas" (331)
(It is not my intention to ever send you these lines to read, for their
sole purpose is to be committed to paper [342]). It is through writing
that Mariana has gained strength, for in setting her emotions down
on paper, she has succeeded in transferring them to another entity—
the blank page—by which she can analyze and ultimately understand
and overcome them. Writing, then, serves as a kind of therapy, forcing
Mariana back into herself to examine her own feelings and emotions.
As a self-reflexive literary form, the epistle allows her to record her reactions to her separation and isolation. And the fact that she is isolated enhances her reactions to the forces that keep her so. For
Mariana, then, this self-conscious process of self-examination, as represented by this new letter, is ultimately more important than communicating with anyone on the outside.[5]

Unlike *Lettres Portugaises,* which contains only the letters written
by Mariana to Bouton, *Novas Cartas Portuguesas* also contains correspondences between Mariana and family members and friends, as well
as letters written to her by Bouton. By breaking with the traditional
narrative format in this fashion, *Novas Cartas Portuguesas* becomes a
"decentered" text in two ways: it lacks both an individual author and a
single protagonist. In *Lettres Portugaises,* the voice of Mariana unifies
the experience of the reader, but in *Novas Cartas Portuguesas,* we hear
a number of voices, mostly of women, many of whom have either only
a first name—Mariana, Maria Ana, Maria, Monica—or no name at
all. In this sense, the book is a history of women's voices articulating
their plight as women in a male-dominated society. That the Three
Marias elected to maintain anonymity was therefore not only a political strategy whereby no one of them could be singled out and prosecuted, but also an effective literary device in keeping with their
meaning. It enhanced and augmented the polyphonic nature of the
book, so that what is heard is a chorus of voices raised in protest.

Among the many voices, of particular interest is the exchange of letters between Mariana and her childhood friend Joana, who is now married. Their correspondence reveals that, although Mariana is physically confined within the convent, Joana, who was forced into a marriage without love, suffers restraints and deprivation which in many ways rival those of convent life. Joana writes, among other things, that she is unable to conceive a child for which she is rebuked and scorned by those around her. While lamenting their powerless condition as women, Mariana sees in Joana's barren state a silent victory over the forces that condemn them to a life of misery:

> Vingança é tua esterilidade, desforra; por ela te negas a ser utilizada: mãe te tornando de homem ou mulher gerados por marido que odeias. Fêmea para dar crias: filho varão que siga a casta, em montada e nome do pai ... a isso te recusas pelo útero, em tua revolta, Joana, e abençoada sejas! (185)

> Your barrenness is revenge, just retribution; it permits you to refuse to be used: to become the mother of a man or a woman fathered by a husband that you hate, to be merely a woman to breed sons on: male offspring continuing the family line, astride their mounts, in the name of the father ... you have expressed your rebellion by way of your womb, you have refused this, Joana, and blessed be your name! (201)

The letters and poems written by the chevalier to Mariana are an equally interesting departure from the original text which inspired them. In *Lettres Portugaises* there are no letters from Bouton; the nun merely imagines his responses in order to prolong her one-way communication. Thus, she "complains about his indifference, imagines his rebuke, and asks pardon. She plays both parts, providing for herself the cavalier's possible responses and then answers them" (Perry, 1980, 102). The new letters and poems by the chevalier in *Novas Cartas Portuguesas* are significant not only as a break from tradition, but also as further proof of the disabling effect of society's strictures. Although Mariana suffers the separation and isolation imposed upon women, the writings of the chevalier reveal that men, too, can be victims of a system that forces them to assume roles of power and action, leaving them to reconcile these roles with the feelings of despair, loss, and abandonment generally accorded women in fateful love affairs. As a result, the language of the chevalier's letters and poems in the

contemporary work is not at all typical of the soldier-lover figure of
conventional romance, nor does it resemble the words placed in the
mouth of the chevalier by the Mariana of *Lettres Portugaises*. Instead,
the chevalier makes an ironic complaint, remarking that Mariana has
come out on top: in making public her side of their love affair in the
now internationally renowned *Lettres Portugaises*, she has achieved
her goal of becoming a celebrated writer and a woman of the world.
Elsewhere *Novas Cartas Portuguesas* contains letters by fictional de-
scendants of Mariana Alcoforado who criticize what they consider to
be the ploys and falsehoods that Bouton resorts to in telling his side of
the story—as if the different authors of the book were debating about
the political wisdom of including such material. Ultimately, however,
the chevalier's letters do not diminish the central issue of oppression.
On the contrary, his words, as well as those of other men in the book
(like Mariana's cousin, José Maria, whose despair at having lost
Mariana to the convent and his wife to another man and then to suicide, finally leads to his own suicide) merely suggest that the repressions of women can also damage men, especially in their roles as
husbands, lovers, fathers, and sons.

The isolation, abandonment, grief, and despair reflected in the
lives of these men and women from an earlier period in history reappear in the correspondence of a more contemporary generation: in a
letter from a woman, Mariana, to her husband who left Portugal to
work in a remote area of Canada nine years earlier; in a letter from a
university student named Mariana to her boyfriend who fled Portugal
to avoid being drafted and sent to Africa to ensure imperial domina-
tion there; and in numerous other missives by women who, through
letter writing, are either struggling to cope with the patriarchy or are
defying it. In the epistles exchanged among the Three Marias, which
appear intermittently throughout the text, the same problems and
concerns are reiterated. Like their predecessors, they turn to writing
as a form of protest and release in a world which has successfully kept
woman contained by the walls of a convent, by the walls of their
homes, or by the more problematical, invisible walls formed by the
patriarchy.

As the starting point of their collaborative project, as well as the
central thread weaving in and out of the poems, fictitious letters, essays, and other entries in the book, the letters exchanged among the
authors are of special import. Grouped under the headings "First Let-

ter," "Second Letter," and "Third Letter," these nonfictional letters are also consecutively numbered ("First Letter I," "Second Letter I," "Third Letter I," "First Letter II," and so on), indicating their chronology within their respective sets. The only requirements that the authors imposed upon themselves in writing the book were to reveal how much the three women were aware of the appropriateness of the epistle to their cause. This literary mode, perhaps better than any other, connotes the very conditions that prompted them as women to write the book: isolation, separation, despair, seemingly insurmountable obstacles, and a struggle toward unity. And if the epistle was the best means of expressing their social conditions, other characteristics of the form were equally well suited to their narrative purposes. For example, in epistolary fiction the formal unities of time and place are frequently absent. As Ruth Perry points out in her study of epistolary prose:

> One effect of telling stories about the consciousness of the characters is that it gives a continuous sense of time even when there is no formal unity of time or place in this genre. The reader soon disregards the formal dislocations and paces himself instead to the inward rhythms of the epistolary characters who are always reacting to the present. (Perry 1980, 120)

The fact that, in addition to their own letters, the Three Marias were writing whatever they wanted in whatever form they elected made the epistle a desirable form. For like the epistolary novel, *Novas Cartas Portuguesas* does not rely on a sequence of events or characters' actions; its plot is derived from the characters' sustained evaluation of themselves and the recording and transmission of their thoughts to one another. Still another factor favoring the epistolary form has to do with the temporal quality of immediacy it connotes. In writing about events of the past, as in an autobiography or memoir, authors tend to shape and trim their account according to their knowledge of the final results (Perry 1980, 120). But the Three Marias were interested in documenting events as they lived through them (the writing of the book is one such event). The primacy of the epistolary form for this purpose is evident since it allows them to comment on events as they occur. Moreover, in their attempt to raise the consciousness of others with regard to the plight of women in society, the letter was especially suitable, for not only could they record their immediate experiences as women and writers, they could draw the reader into living these experiences as well.

The distribution of these letters, like all other entries in the text, was determined by their date of composition. Of the twenty-four letters exchanged among the three writers, more than half appear in the first third of the book. A few appear sporadically throughout the remainder of the text until the very end, where four occupy the final pages. In order to understand better this rather lopsided distribution, it is first necessary to elaborate on the attitudes held by these women at the time they were writing.

As Helen Lane points out in the preface to her English translation, what was clear from the very onset of the project was that, although the Three Marias were in agreement in their willingness to challenge the injustices and restrictions imposed upon women, they were not unified in their perceptions about the cause or root of the problem of women's oppression. Barreno felt that the institution of motherhood was the prime oppressor; Horta believed that society in general victimized women, but that men in particular and especially men as husbands, lovers, fathers, and sons were women's most formidable oppressors. Velho da Costa, unlike the other two, was not a militant feminist, and she felt that some women could be as overbearing as men. She believed that men as well as women were victims, a belief perhaps best articulated by the fictitious letters written from the chevalier to the nun.

The fact that the first third of the book is heavily populated by their nonfictional letters suggests the Three Marias need to establish at once a dialogue and a polemic centering on the nature and causes of women's oppression. In these letters they register their reactions and their agreements and disagreements regarding the condition of women while, simultaneously, questioning themselves and the other two as to how to combat this oppression. The initial flood of the nonfictional letters, then, not only sets the tone of the work, which is at once political, social, economic, and historical; but also functions as a forum for raising key issues concerning them as women and writers. And these issues—including the writing of subversive material, the need for sisterhood, the struggle toward self-understanding through writing, and the invention of positive role models for women—subsequently resurface as themes in the various other entries in the

book. Once these basic concerns have been articulated in the beginning, the letters exchanged between the authors become less frequent
until the very end. This decline or lull in their three-way dialogue coincides with the authors' need to expand the scope and body of the
book from the stories of three contemporary women to include the arguments, outcries, and testimonies of other women and men who, like
them, suffer from the social system. And they do this by adopting a
variety of fictional and nonfictional modes which tell the stories of
countless women and men from generations past and present. In one
of the final letters exchanged, one of the Three Marias remarked that
the most important and rewarding parts of the book were those in
which they, as writers, lose themselves in the minds and bodies of
these different literary personae, whose individual stories are, in many
ways, more profound and meaningful to their cause than the comments and reactions contained in the personal letters.

Novas Cartas Portuguesas ends as it begins with the authors' nonfictional letters. A close study of these final letters shows that, although the women are united in their stance against the repressive
dictates of society, they remain divided in their individual interpreta-
tions of the causes of oppression. In other words, their letters to one
another, as a unifying textual device, give shape to their common
concerns as well as to their disunity. It should be noted that following their arrest and trial, Velho da Costa wrote a letter to a Portuguese newspaper disassociating herself from the other two with
regard to their feminist involvements, and she criticized the feminist
movement for having transformed the book into a banner for their
cause. As mentioned earlier, her view of oppression was not limited
to the problems of women alone, rather to the problems of all those
who find themselves, because of race, class, or gender, victims of the
dominant culture.

Hence, one of the most important points to be made about *Novas
Cartas Portuguesas* as radical literature is that it avoids a meta-
language or a master discourse which would control the meaning of
the text, thus remaining open in a way that few political arguments
and few narratives are. Consider, for example, how the authors have
treated the problem of narrative organization. In their attempt to find
a form in which they could talk about women's issues and social injustices, the Three Marias have rejected not only the Bildungsroman but
also the typical feminist-modernist narrative, which, in place of an

action-oriented plot, offers its mirror image—a progression of
thoughts, emotions, and dreams often described as the "voyage in."
Their own book does not close with the kind of divine coming-to-
awareness that these two kinds of novels promote. In fact, there is no
closure in *Novas Cartas Portuguesas*, no resolution of the various issues, concerns, and conflicting positions. The authors themselves
stated as much in a postscript to the English translation:

> This book is not the work of an isolated writer struggling with personal
> phantoms and problems of expression in order to communicate with an
> abstract Other, nor is it the summing-up of the product of three such
> writers working separately on the same theme. The book is the *written
> record* of a much broader, common, lived experience of creating a sister-
> hood through conflict, shared fun and sorrow, complicity and
> competition—an interplay not only of modes of writing but of modes
> of being, some of them conscious and some far less so, all of them shift-
> ing in the process, and all three of us still facing, even today, the ques-
> tion of *how*. (Quoted in Lane 1975, 399)

Thus, the Three Marias' *Novas Cartas Portuguesas* challenges many
of the basic assumptions underlying the politics of representation in
Western society. The book is charged with dissent against an established order, defined in this case as the patriarchy, and it inevitably
needs to explore modes of writing other than those traditionally sanctioned or offered as models by the literary establishment. Partly as a
result of their working conditions and partly as a result of this need to
discover a new form, the Three Marias have developed a polyphonic,
decentered text which seems to generate from no single author, which
has a more complex temporal order than the linear narrative of the
romantic-realist tradition, and which has no definite closure. Although their book retains a narrative interest, it abandons the typical
novelistic concern with a story about the growth of an individual in
society; instead, it devises a form that illustrates a broad range of historical developments and a variety of social determinants. Relying on
fictional and nonfictional modes, the authors reject the notion of the
individual as the center of the universe as well as the notion that social struggle can ever come to an end. Theirs is a "story" which is unresolved, as their above statement and the continued debates by
feminists and others attest.

NOTES

1. In addition to Helen R. Lane's translation of *The Three Marias: New Portuguese Letters* (1975), Mary Lyndon Fonseca's article "The Case of the Three Marias" (1975) was especially responsible for bringing *Novas Cartas Portuguesas* to the attention of the American audience. Their works in particular supplied me with much of the historical information for my discussion of the events surrounding the publication of the book.

2. Translations are by Helen R. Lane from *The Three Marias: New Portuguese Letters* (1975).

3. Virginia Woolf comments on the long-standing association between women and letters in her essay on the seventeenth-century writer Dorothy Osborne and her *Letters*:

> The art of letter-writing is often the art of essay-writing in disguise. But such as it was, it was an art that a woman could practice without unsexing herself. It was an art that could be carried on at odd moments, by a father's sick bed, among a thousand interruptions, without exciting comment, anonymously as it were, and often with the pretense that it served some useful purpose. (Woolf 1967, 60)

4. I found Ruth Perry, *Letters, Women, and the Novel* (1980) to be invaluable for background on the epistolary novel and insightful in its remarks on *Lettres Portugaises*.

5. See Perry 1980, pp. 119–35, for an in-depth treatment of the self-reflexive aspect of epistolary prose.

II

MODERNISM AND FEMINISM IN FERNANDA BOTELHO'S XERAZADE E OS OUTROS

After the revolution of 1974, a substantial body of feminist literature began to appear in Portugal, much of which was indirectly inspired by the 1972 publication of the controversial *Novas Cartas Portuguesas*. It would be a mistake, however, to think that feminist consciousness lay completely dormant during the repressive Salazar-Caetano dictatorship, emerging only with the Three Marias and the subsequent revolution. Consider the case of Fernanda Botelho, a relatively neglected but impressive poet and novelist whose major work of fiction, *Xerazade e os Outros* (Scheherazade and the Others) (1964), is an intriguing blend of modernist experiment with proto-feminist themes.

If the ideological significance of Botelho's novel has gone unnoticed, that is perhaps because the period from 1950 to 1965 was not an especially liberated time in Portugal and because Botelho, who has recently published her first novel after sixteen years of silence, has never claimed to be a spokesperson for women under patriarchy.[1] At first glance, in fact, *Xerazade e os Outros* seems to be concerned more with the typical issues of literary modernism than with any kind of social rebellion. It is a fragmented, self-reflexive text, filled with parallels between classical myth and contemporary life, narrated from multiple viewpoints, seemingly preoccupied with aesthetic form rather than with women's oppression. And yet, looked at more closely, the novel becomes a subtle, powerful account of the tragic position of a certain type of middle-class woman in Portuguese society. It prefigures many later feminist works, and is an interesting example of how modernist techniques can contribute to a critique of social institutions.

Botelho's fusion of modernism and a nascent feminism becomes evident if we consider how she uses the myth of Scheherazade to give order and meaning to her novel. Scheherazade is, after all, a symbol of the female storyteller—a fictional character whose tales of adventure were so cleverly constructed that they won her her survival. The story of Scheherazade—a woman who jeopardized her own well-being to end a reign of terror over women—therefore has feminist implications. Daughter of the sultan's executioner, Scheherazade offered herself in marriage to the sultan in the hope that she could halt his daily marrying and subsequent murdering of women in the realm—a practice he put into effect after having discovered that his first wife was unfaithful. Scheherazade's plan was to invite her sister to the bridal chamber where the sister would request that Scheherazade tell her one last story. Secure in her skill as a storyteller, Scheherazade was convinced that she could postpone her own execution by entertaining her husband with a series of tales, each of which she would leave unresolved until the following evening. So successful was she in spinning her tales, that the sultan not only stayed her execution for 1001 nights, but also renounced his need to marry and kill other women in order to avenge his honor. Scheherazade remained his wife, and they purportedly lived happily ever after.

Botelho is not the first woman writer to employ this myth. Isak Dinesen, for example, liked to compare herself to Scheherazade, emphasizing her ability to captivate her listening audience for hours on end. But whereas Dinesen romanticized the myth and repeatedly served a male audience, Botelho tends to reveal the dark, ironic implications of Scheherazade's role. For in *Xerazade e os Outros*, storytelling, like feminine attractiveness, is seen as something of a curse—a condition imposed on women who must fabricate fictions for male audiences in order to survive.

By subtitling *Xerazade e os Outros* "Romance (Tragédia em Forma de)" (Novel [Tragedy in the Form of]) Botelho explicitly links the notion of classical tragedy to the myth and also opens up the possibility of using a purely dramatic form alongside the narrative powers of a novel. One thinks again of the comment by Virginia Woolf, who, in *A Room of One's Own*, observed that women writers preferred the novel to drama and poetry, since it was still a relatively new and pliable form. Woolf was convinced that contemporary women authors would not only reshape the novel, but would also modify traditional genres: "And I went on to ponder how a woman nowadays would write a poetic tragedy in 5 acts. Would she use verse?—would she not use prose rather?" (Woolf 1967, 116). Whether or not Botelho was aware of Woolf's remark (or of Woolf's *The Waves*, 1931, which is like a novel, but which draws upon conventions of theatrical soliloquy and techniques of lyric poetry), she seems to have felt a similar discontent with established literary forms, and her attempt to escape traditional generic distinctions is homologous with her interest in revealing the unhappy condition of women.

In the last analysis, I should emphasize that Botelho is not a self-consciously feminist writer. Indeed, her use of the Scheherazade myth and her structural manipulation of devices from classical tragedy are signs of a somewhat contradictory attitude which modernist literature often took toward bourgeois culture: it tried to pose alternative values, but frequently it moved back to the old, predemocratic world to seek a model for what the new literature should become.[2] Botelho's novel is therefore both similar to and very different from a later, more politically radical work like *Novas Cartas Portuguesas*. On the one hand, it gives a vivid picture of the condition of middle-class women in pre-revolutionary Portugal, evincing a desire to break from established forms of literature; on the other hand, it stops short of being an openly committed or didactic text.

These implications will become more apparent if we consider the novel in detail, beginning with its unusual form, which suggests that Botelho herself wanted to stop playing Scheherazade. She does not appear before us in the guise of the conventional storyteller, giving the sultan his pleasure; instead, she forces us to *work* at the production of meaning and, in the process, threatens to deconstruct novelistic discourse. Ultimately, *Xerazade e os Outros* has a great deal in common with ordinary realist fiction; nevertheless, it is an unusual book for its day—it reveals indirectly the problems of women, linking those problems to the theme of writing or storytelling, and remarkably anticipates the later, post-structuralist concern with relations between gender and representation.

Xerazade e os Outros is divided into three principal sections that are not like the conventional chapters of a novel, nor are they quite like the acts of a drama. The titles of these sections—"Coro I" (Chorus I), "Personagens" (Characters), and "Cenas" (Scenes)—seem to represent largely nonlinear categories. Within each section, the author appears to be more concerned with rendering thoughts and actions simultaneously than with constructing a plot; thus, although a narrative situation gradually emerges from the text, it is always tentative, estranged by the unusual technique.

The first section of the book, "Coro I," is subdivided into five parts of approximately equal length. Like the chorus in classical tragedy, it is designed to introduce the central characters; however, although the dramatic chorus speaks with a single voice, the chorus in *Xerazade e os Outros* is individualized, composed of several secondary figures in the story, each of whom sets the stage by providing indirect information about the principal actors. Furthermore, whereas the classical chorus has a decidedly rhetorical function—commenting on the themes of the play and providing help to the audience—Botelho's chorus is disorienting. Within the five sections of "Coro I," the reader is presented with a series of seemingly unrelated voices, most of which have only a first name or no name at all; they, in turn, comment on various characters who are identified only by a nickname or some other vague reference, such as "o lorde" (the lord) and "uma velha" (an old woman). These choral voices, which speak only to one another, never give the reader the basic information he or she needs to normalize the action; moreover, the settings change bewilderingly from section to section.

An example of Botelho's oddly individualized yet anonymous treatment of the chorus can be found in the opening lines of the book, which introduce one of the story's principal characters:

—Aí vem a nossa Xerazade!—disse um.
—A Xerazadezinha!—confirmou o outro.
—E que linda vem a nossa Xerazade!—murmurou um terceiro.
A quarta personagem ergueu timidamente os olhos e segredou, como em êxtase que a si próprio causava alguma surpresa—e aos outros mereceu irónica reserva:—Xerazade! (Botelho 1964, 11)

"Here comes our Scheherazade!" said one.
"Little Scheherazade!" confirmed the other.
"And look how pretty our Scheherazade is!" murmured a third.
The fourth character timidly raised his eyes and whispered with such ecstasy that it even surprised himself—and was viewed by the others with an ironic reserve: "Scheherazade!"

In this first section, considerable attention is given to describing the movements of the individual called Xerazade, but the identity of the four men who observe and comment on her is vague, indicated either by a kind of numerical distinction, as seen above, or by a more generalized, collective terminology such as *parceiros* (partners), *acólitos* (acolytes), and *personagens* (characters). In the subsequent four sections of "Coro I," similar techniques keep all of the characterizations limited and ill-defined, as if Botelho were concerned only with broad features of social class and gender and with an attenuated, fragmented narrative structure. In the first section, four men watch and discuss the actions of Xerazade; in the second part, an irascible doorman gossips about the apparent improprieties going on between a young fellow and a girl who works in a *tabacaria* (tobacco shop) across the street; in part three, a maid tells a friend about her visit to the house of a wealthy gentleman where she is seeking employment; in part four, two secretaries gossip about the boss' wife; and in the final section, two young boys taunt an old woman passing by in the street. There is no cause and effect relationship between the different sections. Each one seems to involve a different story, beginning in media res and withholding closure. Indeed, because there is no cause and effect relationship between the sections, and since each section has its own cast of characters and distinct setting, they could be read in virtually any order without disrupting or disturbing the whole.

At first glance, the second part ("Personagens") seems as confusing as the first part, primarily because the characters and situations are now seen from different points of view. Many of the characters remain the same, but their names are different; it is left to the reader to identify "Berto," "Carlos," "Luísa" and "Tia Vina"—all of whom appeared in the first part, where they are known by nicknames and other references used by the chorus. Structural parallels between the first two parts help make the process of identification easier and, at the same time, allow a sense of plot to emerge from the apparently random fragments of the book. Like "Coro I," "Personagens" is divided into five sections (in this case, monologues are interspersed with some dialogue), and each section bears as its title a name or expression used by the chorus to refer to one of the principal characters. The order of these sections corresponds to the series of character portraits offered by the chorus in "Coro I." For example, in the first section of "Coro I," the character known as Xerazade is observed; in the corresponding section of "Personagens," she speaks her own monologue, identifying herself as Luísa. Similarly, the young fellow at the *tabacaria,* described in the second section of "Coro I," is the speaker called Berto in part two of "Personagens." The third, fourth, and fifth sections follow a similar pattern: the wealthy gentleman in part three of the chorus is the "Big Boss" (Luísa's husband, Carlos); the public relations man is Gil; and the old woman, who appears in the final section of the "Coro I," reappears as Tia Vina, Luísa's aunt, in the final section of "Personagens."[3]

Although the book's title calls attention to the importance of Xerazade to the story, the multiple viewpoints and disconnected fragments in part 1 and 2 seem to discourage the emergence of a single character. What is presented in these two parts can perhaps be more appropriately described as an ensemble, or as a group of individuals whose lives and experiences are intertwined. Notice too that, like "Coro I," "Personagens" does not rely upon a strong sense of narrative cause and effect. The first section, "Xerazade," records the thoughts of Luísa as she leaves a café and returns home to find that her husband has unexpectedly returned from a business trip and is in consultation with Gil, his public relations man; in "O Pobre Diabo" (The Poor Devil), Berto describes his unsuccessful attempt to meet Luísa in the café; and in "O Big Boss," Carlos ponders the events of the day, his working relationship with Gil and others, and his marriage to Luísa as he, Gil, and, then later, Luísa exchange pleasantries following her return home. "O Public Relations," told from Gil's point of view, is perhaps the most complex of all the monologues; it focuses on Gil's attraction to Luísa and his fascination with storytelling. Finally, "Uma Velha Tinha um Gato" (An Old Woman Had a Cat), the concluding section, presents the rather disconnected thoughts of Luísa's aunt Vina, whose life revolves around Luísa, her lodger Berto, her cat Saturno, and various other people and events from the past. Because these five monologues are concerned with the same people and events, as seen from different points of view, their overall impression is one of simultaneity rather than progression.

The sense of a slightly decentered narrative with indefinite origins and no clear ending is maintained in the third and final section of the book, "Cenas," which consists of a series of nine consecutively numbered scenes and a subsection entitled "Coro II." Nevertheless, a more traditionally novelistic pattern begins to emerge, and the character Luísa becomes a sort of protagonist for the fiction. The sequence of corresponding character descriptions, established in "Coro I" and "Personagens," does not extend to this section; "Cenas" gives a much greater sense of temporal progress. The section opens with a scene between Luísa and Carlos, who are spending the evening at home. Their words to one another, interspersed with strained silences, result in Luísa's leaving the house and subsequently meeting Gil, who has taken an American client, Mr. Richardson, to the casino. Mr. Richardson (whose name ironically recalls the author of *Clarissa*) showers Luísa with much unwanted attention; finally, after several rounds of drinks, Gil and Luísa take the inebriated American back to his hotel and proceed to another club, where Luísa becomes increasingly drunk. After leaving the bar, they stop at a small, dingy restaurant for something to eat. Luísa suffers a kind of mental breakdown at the restaurant, whereupon Gil decides to take her to her aunt's house. In the final scene, Luísa tells her husband, who has come to take her home, that their relationship is over, and he leaves without her.

The action in "Cenas" tends to shift rapidly from one place to another, like cross-cutting in a film. While Luísa is fighting off the attentions of Mr. Richardson in the casino, Carlos is waiting for her to return home, intermittently calling her aunt and threatening not to take Luísa back if she doesn't return shortly. For a while the story weaves back and forth between Luísa, Gil, and Mr. Richardson in the casino and Carlos at home and on the telephone; then it moves to Berto, who has returned home to find Tia Vina hysterical, fearing for Luísa's safety and her marriage. By constantly changing the point of view in this way, Botelho calls attention to the connections and contrasts between the different characters as the events of the evening unfold. At one moment the narrative takes the form of a monologue by Berto, who is searching the bars around town for Luísa; and at another moment, the focus shifts to a monologue by Tia Vina, whose thoughts dart back and forth between the past—a time which for her

has become more real than the present—and the frightening concerns of the moment, especially Luísa's inexplicable actions and the
threatening telephone calls from Carlos.

The unexpected shifts from one character to another help to establish a web of relations among people. In the fourth scene, for example,
Luísa, Gil, and Richardson are about to leave the casino:

> —Vamos?—murmura-lhe ele, poisando-lhe com suavidade a mão no
> ombro. Ela estremece e olha-o, suplicante.
> —Aos fados—esclarece o Gil.
> —Aos fados?
> —Aos fados, sim, minha querida!
> —Sim, ouvi. Aos fados. Vamos lá aos fados.
> Mas não se ergue imediatamente. Tremem-lhe as mãos ao agarrar a
> carteira. "Vamos!" sussurra Gil. Ela volta a olhá-lo e, desta vez, levanta-
> se, levanta-se lentamente, muito lentamente.
> Ele estende-lhe um braço como a indicar-lhe o caminho, o caminho
> onde Mr. Richardson os espera, jovial. O outro braço aflora-lhe as
> costas, impelindo-a docemente, lentamente ... (198–99)

> "Shall we go?" he murmurs, gently placing his hand on her shoulder.
> She trembles and looks at him imploringly.
> "To the fados (folksongs)," Gil explains.
> "To the fados?"
> "Yes, to the fados, my dear!"
> "Yes, I heard. To the fados. Let's go to the fados."
> But she doesn't get up immediately. Her hands tremble as she picks
> up her wallet. "Let's go!" Gil whispers. She turns and looks at him, and
> this time, she raises herself, getting up slowly, very slowly.
> He gives her his arm, as if to show her the way at the end of which Mr.
> Richardson waits for them jovially. His other arm lightly touches her
> back, pushing her forward sweetly, slowly ...

A small space on the page separates this paragraph from the next,
which begins as follows:

> Desliza na semiobscuridade, ziguezagueando por entre as mesas,
> curvado (para não tirar a vista), inoportuno, provocando um
> desarrumo temporário, um arrastar múltiplo de cadeiras, um rodar de
> mesas uma após outra.... Quando ele passa, um copo tomba, uma
> dama inclina-se para apanhar um gancho, alguém protesta "ora, ora!

Há gente realmente que não tem um mínimo de . . ." Ele refugia-se na
sua indiferença, olhando acima do mar de cabeças, sempre em frente.
(199)
    He glides in the semidarkness, zigzagging between tables, bent over
(so as not to distract his gaze), a bit clumsy, causing a temporary confusion, the scooting of several chairs, a circling of tables one after the
other. . . . When he passes by, a glass falls, a woman leans over to pick
up a hairpin, someone shouts, "Well now! There are some people who
don't have the slightest . . ." He withdraws into his own indifference,
his gaze skimming the sea of heads, always directed forwards.

The description of someone walking around tables in a dimly lighted
club appears at first to be a continuation of the action in the preceding paragraph. A bit further along, however, we discover that the description has nothing to do with either Gil or Richardson (as the
pronoun *ele* [he] might suggest). In fact, the entire scene has shifted
to Berto, who is weaving around some tables in a bar in search of
Luísa. Here the narration depicts the simultaneous actions of characters in two different situations, and their movements tend to mirror
one another.
    Not only the characters' movements but also their thoughts tend to
overlap. For example, in the eighth scene, Berto returns home to tell
Tia Vina of his unsuccessful attempt to locate Luísa. His description,
detailing a near encounter with her in a bar, is interrupted in
midsentence by a long, rambling monologue which, although never
indicated specifically in the text, is spoken by Luísa:

    Não sei se ria, se chore. É o fado, é isso, ó meu homem, é isso. O fado
bole-me. . . . Não, não quero o fado, não quero. Tira daí essa porcaria,
não quero o fado. . . . Hã!? Café? Dizes que é café? Pois não quero, não
quero café nem fado, o café bole-me, tudo me bole, tu boles-me, nem
sei porquê, mas boles-me, tudo me bole, isto aqui, as mesas ali, e aquela
pilha de chocolates. . . . Paga lá o que quiseres, meu homem—a
chávena, o pires, tudo! O patrão paga. Que limpe, que limpe! Sou uma
lady, diz-lho. Parto a loiça, parto os chocolates, parto-lhe a cara, parto,
parto, parto . . . ! (248–249)

    I don't know whether to laugh or cry. It's the fado, it's that, my fel-
low, it's that. Fado gets to me. . . . No, I don't want fado, I don't want it.
Take that crap out of here, I don't want fado. Huh? Coffee? You say it's

coffee? Well I don't want it, I don't want coffee or fado. Coffee gets to
me, everything gets to me, you get to me, I don't know why, but you get
to me, everything gets to me, this here, the tables there, and that stack
of chocolates.... Pay whatever you want, my man—the cup, the sau-
cer, everything! The boss pays. Clean it up, clean it up! I'm a lady, tell
him. I'll smash the china, the chocolates, I'll smash your face, smash,
smash, smash ... !

Luísa's confused and troubled state of mind, exacerbated by her
drunken spree, is depicted by disconnected and nonsensical words, ultimately giving way to a desperate, crazed peal of laughter:

> ... Ó meu homem, tira-me o amarelo e os chocolates e esta cabeça de
> cebo que limpa, limpa, limpa.... É uma montanha de coisas, e todas
> mexem, e todas cheiram, e todas bolem ... amarelo, azedo, carrascão,
> cebo, cebo, fado, fado, pernas nuas, pêlo ruivo, imagens, imagens,
> imagens, alho, alho, senhor Borralho!, imagens.... Oh! tudo frito em
> azeite ... alho, alho, senhor Borralho! Ah!-ah!-ah! (249)

> ... Oh my man, take away the yellow and the chocolates and this fat
> head that cleans, cleans, cleans.... It's a mountain of things, and
> they're all moving, and they all smell, they're moving ... yellow, sour,
> cheap wine, fat, fat, fado, fado, bare legs, red hair, images, images, im-
> ages, garlic, garlic, Mr. Borr [garlic], images.... Oh! everything fried in
> oil ... garlic, garlic, Mr. Borr [garlic]! Ha! ha! ha!

To reinforce the simultaneity of Berto and Luísa's words and
thoughts, the narrative shifts back to Berto's description of the evening, and his sentence ("O homem que veio abrir ..." [248] [The
man who came to open ...]), which was abruptly interrupted by
Luísa's words, is completed in the first line of the paragraph following
her monologue (" ... era um homem das cavernas, parecia mesmo
saído duma caverna" [250] [... was a cave man, he actually seemed
to have come out of a cave]). Berto's story also helps to explain
Luísa's troubled state of mind: in recounting the events of the evening, he tells Vina that one bar owner described Luísa to him, saying
that she was very drunk and that she was at the center of a disturbance
which nearly resulted in his calling the police.

The disconnected scenes, the shifting points of view, and the disorienting nature of certain dialogues and descriptions in "Cenas" are a

variation on and an extension of the unusual structural and stylistic devices that make "Coro I" and "Personagens" such fascinating and, at the same time, bewildering reading. But in "Cenas," Botelho takes an even bolder step by interjecting, just prior to the final scene, "Coro II," which is unlike any other section of the book. Narrated from a third-person point of view, "Coro II" introduces the author, who has momentarily interrupted the writing of the book to speak:

—E agora, Saturno?—também pergunta o Autor do Romance (Tragédia em Forma de), com a natural desenvoltura dos que assistem, dos que apenas assistem—desalienados, programáticos (e pragmáticos, se quiserem!), tão afetivos do real quotidiano como intolerantes da realidade onírica. (253)

"And now, Saturn?" also asks the Author of the Novel (Tragedy in the Form of), with the natural boldness of those who observe, of those who merely observe—unalienated, programmatic (and pragmatic, if you wish!), as enamored of the day-to-day actuality as they are intolerant of oneiric reality.

"Coro II" presents us with a brief, detached, inconclusive meditation on the characters and situations in the book, on the relationship between reality and imagination, and on the creative process in general.[4] In some ways, it resembles a Brechtian device that breaks the illusion of the world represented in the novel, but it also has a second, more subtle implication. Botelho suggests that the voice of the author—whether implied or explicit—is as much a convention as the characters and scenes in the book; indeed, she makes her authorial persona seem like a character or a mask, using the masculine form to designate "his" voice. Instead of placing this authorial voice outside the fictional world and giving it privileged status, she sets it apart reducing it to a component of the text, equivalent to the other speakers. In this way, she verges on a truly radical technique that has something in common with the "authorless" texts of the postmodern avant-garde. At the same time, consciously or not, she makes her role as writer seem ironic—rather like a dramatic masquerade governed by a patriarchal law.

Xerazade e os Outros departs from the conventions of narrative realism in many ways. Ultimately, however, it reveals the outlines of a traditional sort of plot, and this plot has an interesting relation to Botelho's technique. The shadowy, indistinct story Botelho tells is in one sense typical of feminist literature; compare, for example, Kate Chopin's *The Awakening,* which deals with a woman's dissatisfaction with her role as wife and mother and her ultimate break with her husband and her lover-friend, who has been instrumental in bringing about her "awakening." Like Chopin's work, *Xerazade e os Outros* articulates the confusion, fear, and solitude of a woman striving to cope with the world around her. Luísa's nickname, "Xerazade," is pertinent to this feminist theme, foregrounding the issue of women and survival. It draws a parallel between Luísa and Scheherazade in the sense that, like her legendary storyteller-sister, Luísa's success and well-being in society depend on her ability to fascinate and entertain men. But whereas Scheherazade was skillful with words, Luísa must perform with her body, transforming her self into a fiction.

Luísa's nickname, "Xerazade," is also an acknowledgement by her husband's secretaries (as well as others) that she is the boss' third and longest standing wife, and that she has managed to maintain this position by being attractive and alluring, as well as mysterious— qualities which make her appealing not only to Carlos, but also to other men, as the secretaries' innuendos about her relationships with Gil and Berto make quite clear. Throughout, this link with the mythical Scheherazade is grounded in a theatrical rather than a literary metaphor. A dynamic between males and females, based on the principle that men observe while women display themselves for male pleasure, can be seen in the very first pages of the text. The three pages constituting the initial section of "Coro I," which begins with a conversation between four men about a woman, contain more than twenty references to "looking," resulting from the repetition of the words *olho* (eye), *olhos* (eyes), *miradas* (looks), and *olhar* (to look). Thus the anonymous men of the chorus limit their actions to watching, scrutinizing, and commenting on Xerazade and her movements in the café. While their conversation conveys the way they see her—as pretty (*linda*) and as a kind of endearing, fascinating possession ("nossa Xerazadezinha")—the third-person narration allows the reader to study the social practice of men watching women from a more critical distance:

Xerazade vai-se. O braço do criado desfaz o ângulo. Os olhos movem-se no rastro de Xerazade. Os da quarta personagem, outro tanto. E os da terceira, da segunda, da primeira personagem. Cinco pares de olhos no rastro de Xerazade. Até que Xerazade escapa, ilesa não se sabe como, aos cinco pares de olhos. (14)

Scheherazade leaves. The waiter straightens his arm. His eyes follow Scheherazade's trail. The eyes of the fourth character do the same. And those of the third, the second, and the first characters. Five pairs of eyes watching Scheherazade's trail. Until Scheherazade escapes unscathed, one knows not how, by the five pairs of eyes.

These first few pages of the book establish a basic difference between male and female roles in society: men act, in the sense that they look at women, but women appear. The men watching Xerazade in the café have clearly observed her many times because they conjecture whether her friend will meet her there today; furthermore, while watching her, they joke with one another about her "promiscuity," an assumption based upon what they believe to be her illicit meetings with a man whom they know is not her husband. The men's pleasure is voyeuristic, derived solely from watching from a distance a "performance" which is sexually titillating. And while they actively survey Xerazade's gestures and movements, she submits herself to the social demands that teach women to suppress anger or discomfort, watching over themselves as carefully as they are watched by men.

In this first part, we find Xerazade's movements described in a theatrical way:

[A quarta personagem] ficou-se de olhos levantados, cabeça erecta, a seguir, apenas com os olhos, a caprichosa trajectória da notável Xerazade, da porta para o balcão, daí para o telefone, novamente ao balcão, balcão-telefone, agora telefone, compasso de espera, não mais que o tempo regulamentar permitido pela gerência que "aos Exmos. Clientes rogava a fineza de limitar a três minutos a duração das respectivas chamadas."
Pessoa bem comportada, a tímida Xerazade submeteu-se à amável arrogância do regulamento. (11)

[The fourth character] kept his eyes raised, his head erect, following just with his eyes, the capricious trajectory of the remarkable Scheherazade: from the door to the counter, from there to the tele-

phone, back to the counter, counter-telephone, now telephone, waiting, not more than the designated time permitted by the management
that "asked its esteemed customers to kindly limit their respective calls
to three minutes."

A model of deportment, the timid Scheherazade submitted to the
honeyed arrogance of the regulation.

Xerazade is like a figure on a stage, isolated and confined within a pre-
dominantly male space; hence, her movements and gestures are restricted as she walks back and forth between the counter and the
telephone, where she submits to the three-minute limit. Further on in
the narrative, we find her discreetly calling the waiter ("reclama com
discrição a presença do criado" [12]) and nervously spooning sugar
into her coffee while pretending to be calm ("Xerazade está nervosa,
por isso mesmo são lentos, conscientemente lentos, os gestos com que
transporta as colheradas, três, do açucareiro para a chávena,
removendo depois a colher com uma segurança tão pausada que logo
se notava artificial" [12])—all of which suggests her self-
consciousness, her awareness of the fact that she is an object of display. The text also implies that Xerazade is brutalized by the men's
stares, for upon leaving the café, she is described as having somehow
managed to escape "ilesa, não se sabe como, aos cinco pares de olhos"
(14) (unscathed, one knows not how, by the five pairs of eyes).

The difference between men's and women's behavior—the distinction between active looking and passive display—is suggested
throughout the text. In the second section of "Coro I," the sexually
stimulating quality of looking is again suggested. The following description of the doorman Vítor is interesting not only because he is
described as Cerberus, one who is constantly on watch, but also because of the abundance of references to looking and the discreet linking of the notion of looking to the sexual act:

> ... [O magricela] acenou que sim, e desapareceu, rápido, ante o olhar
> crítico, majestoso, do zelador, porteiro para ser mais exacto, ou, para ser
> ainda mais exacto, Cérbero (de quatro andares a dois apartamentos),
> não com três cabeças mas um par de olhos, vivos, atentos, desdobráveis
> em quantos pares de olhos fossem necessários para a total vigilância do
> imóvel, de alto a baixo, esquerdo-direito, intramuros, extramuros,
> olhos promíscuos, absorventes, soberanos. (15)

... [The skinny fellow] nodded yes, and rapidly disappeared before the critical, majestic gaze of the keeper, the doorman, to be more precise, or to be even more precise, Cerberus (with four floors with two apartments each), not with three heads but with a pair of lively and attentive eyes that could multiply themselves into as many as necessary in order to guard the place from top to bottom, left to right, inside, outside, eyes that were promiscuous, all-absorbing, sovereign.

Note, however, the distinction made between men and women in the following passage. While the doorman stares boldly, the maid, who is uncomfortable with looking openly, disguises and restricts her gaze:

[O porteiro] suspendeu o discurso, arregalando o par de olhos disponível, em linha recta, para a tabacaria do outro lado da rua. Perfilou-se, tocado pela cena ultrajante que o par de olhos reconduzia à sua consciência. A mulher seguiu-lhe o olhar, mas de viés, discretamente. (16)

[The doorman] stopped talking, opening wide his unoccupied pair of eyes to look straight ahead at the tobacco shop across the street. He drew himself up, shocked by the outrageous scene that his eyes rerouted to his brain. The woman followed his gaze, but indirectly, discreetly.

The remainder of this section is concerned primarily with the doorman Vítor's fascination with the girl who runs the *tabacaria* across the street. He is convinced that she is too young to be working there, constantly exposed to the improper advances of fast-talking young men, like the one who is speaking to her now. While he condemns the girl's mother, Dona Clotilde, for permitting her daughter to come in contact with such undesirable men, he revels in watching the two figures deep in conversation, and he interprets their behavior as a promiscuous act. Although he is proud of his own moral superiority, he is in fact as much a voyeur as any of the other males in the story; he, too, treats women as spectacles to be watched for a kind of sexual gratification.

The importance given to looking in the relationship between men and women in the first part of the book is reaffirmed in the second part in the opening of the first section, where there are repeated references to seeing and being seen:

Quando um homem me lança na rua um daqueles olhares manho-
sos, provocadores, olhar não precisamente de homem a quem o
respeito por uma senhora impede que, nele, o macho venha à
superfície, eu tenho por força de o esbofetear—pelo menos com o meu
desdém, ou com esta fria majestade que sinto em mim desde há algum
tempo. Que desejaria sentir em mim para poder, como os seres
privilegiados, esbofetear a soberba com que outros se enfeitam perante
as minhas franquezas. Esta majestade com que caminho, vê-me,
contempla-me, admira-me, tu, honesto homem com quem nunca
sonhei, agradeço-te. Levo o teu olhar comigo, levo também o olhar
daquele, sinto que se voltou e me olhou as pernas, as minhas pernas
agradecem-te. E tu, mulherzinha incompetente, admiras talvez os meus
cabelos, porque não lava os teus? Sei que Berto reprovaria os meus
pensamentos, mas não é muito fácil evangelizar-me. Ter-lhe-á
acontecido alguma coisa? Bem roída me sinto por dentro, toda
amachucada, como os meus vestidos de outrora. Sou alguém, duvidam?
... (31)

When a man on the street gives me one of those sly, provoking
looks, not exactly the look of a man whose respect for a lady prevents
the male in him from coming fully to the surface, I must of course
strike him, at least with my disdain, or with this cold majesty that I
have felt within me for some time. A majesty I want to feel in me in
order to strike, like privileged people do, at the pride with which others adorn themselves in the presence of my frankness. This majesty
with which I walk, see me, look at me, admire me, you, honest fellow
of whom I never dreamed, I thank you. I carry your look with me, I
also carry the look of that other fellow over there, I feel that he just
turned around and stared at my legs, my legs thank you. And you, little incompetent woman, do you perhaps admire my hair, why don't
you wash yours? I know that Berto would disapprove of my thoughts,
but it isn't easy to evangelize myself. Could something have happened
to him? I feel all eaten up inside, crumpled, like my old clothes. I am
someone, do you doubt that? ...

Luísa's words indicate her desperation and oppression: constantly
treated as a sexual object, she is aware of being watched and evaluated
by men (as well as by other women), and she knows that this evaluation is critical to her well-being. Her intense dissatisfaction with this
role prompts her to take action. That she does not strike out
(esbofetear) at those who take advantage of her frankness (franqueza)

suggests that she, like most women, is unable to overcome the constraints that keep her silently oppressed. Hence, she is victimized by others and, more importantly, by her own inability to act or react.

In a sense Luísa symbolizes all women who are caught between what they are taught to believe to be their role and purpose in life and what they feel they are or can be in spite of what society dictates. The tragedy of the book stems in part from Luísa's vacillation between the belief that as long as she pleases men she is all right and the realization that she is getting older and must do something in order to survive a system that keeps women of a certain age, especially older single or childless women, marginalized. Thus, at one point in the narrative, Luísa reassures herself that, although she is over thirty, she is still "successful" because men continue to look at her, even though the way they look has somewhat changed: "Cá vou eu com a minha majestade, os homens continuam a olhar-me. O olhar dos homens, esse, ainda não me traiu" (32) (Here I go with my majesty; men continue to look at me. Men's stares, they have yet to betray me). At another moment, however, she senses the gradual decline of her ability to please and fascinate, and she is uncomfortably aware of her husband's increasingly uninterested gaze. She knows that her sense of self is closely tied to her husband's approval, and that his growing lack of interest places her self-esteem as well as her survival in jeopardy:

> E, quando casualmente me vês [Carlos], já no teu olhar é frouxa aquela magnífica perversidade que era o meu orgulho e a minha sobrevivência. (36)

> And when you [Carlos] casually look at me, the magnificent perversity in your eyes, that was my pride and my survival, is now weak.

This is not the first time that Luísa has sensed the decline of her powers to fascinate. Gil, Carlos' employee and Luísa's former boyfriend, introduced her to Carlos because, in her words, he had tired of her: "Talvez por não ser fácil evangelizar-me foi que o Gil me apresentou o Carlos Aloisius, uma forma diplomática de me indicar o seu cansaço" (39) (Perhaps because it was for not being easily evangelized that Gil introduced Carlos Aloisius to me, a diplomatic way of saying he was tired of me). Interestingly, after Luísa marries Carlos, she becomes more desirable to Gil who, in a voyeuristic fashion, prefers to look at her from afar. That Luísa is aware of Gil's attraction to her physical beauty is made clear in the following passage. More interesting, however, is the fact that she sees and evaluates her body in terms of his attraction to it:

> Creio que foi o Gil quem primeiro reparou nos meus joelhos—o que é bem digno dele. É estranho que, ao falar dos meus joelhos ou de qualquer particularidade da minha anatomia, mencionável pelo simples facto de ser bela ("uma forma de pureza," dizia o Gil), os meus pensamentos voem, em primeiro lugar, para o Gil. (38)

> I think it was Gil who first noticed my knees—which is quite worthy of him. It's strange that whenever my knees or any other part of my anatomy comes up in a conversation, simply because it's beautiful ("a form of purity," Gil said), my thoughts first turn to Gil.

In thinking back on their relationship, Luísa recalls Gil's words to her, which reassure her of her physical appeal, but nevertheless disclose the fact that his fascination is based solely on her body—a "thing" which is to be seen and not heard:

> . . . *Perfeito, Luísa! Em qualquer sentido, tu és uma expressão de arte pura, tal como estás, a coisa mais subjectiva que eu conheço, NÃO FALES!, assim mesmo, nua, silenciosa e apenas nos meus olhos . . . (55)*

> . . . *Perfect, Luísa! You are in every sense an expression of pure art, just as you are, the most subjective thing that I know. DON'T SPEAK! Stay as you are, naked, silent, and for my eyes alone . . .*

Since physical possession ironically diminishes her appeal for him, Gil "gives" Luísa to Carlos, who, in turn, marries her—not because he finds her compatible, but because as a possession, an object, she enhances his own sense of self. In "O Big Boss," Carlos admits that his former girlfriend Cristina was more his type and that, had she not run away with another man, he probably would have married her instead of Luísa. What becomes increasingly clear in "O Big Boss" is that Carlos does not understand or care to understand Luísa: "A Maria Luísa, pelo menos, não tem complexos. Note-se: caso os tenha, não dou por eles" (96) (Maria Luísa doesn't have any complexes. Note: in case she has them, I don't pay any attention to them). Throughout, his assessments of Luísa are superficial, based solely on what he sees, even though he indirectly acknowledges that they might be false: "A Cristina é que me convinha. Na minha idade. . . . Note-se: a Maria Luísa é mais submissa. Aparentemente, pelo menos" (96) (Cristina was more suitable for me. At my age. . . . Note: Maria Luísa is more submissive. Apparently so, at least).

Although their relationship has changed to the point where Carlos is no longer fascinated, he is reluctant to dispose of her. As he himself admits, he is not getting any younger. But getting rid of her would also mean losing what he prizes most about Luísa and, in a way, the only thing he values about her—her beautiful skin:

> Quando bem calhe, se houver motivo (e eu estiver na disposição de acatar o motivo, claro!), dá-se um pontapé na terceira esposa, e adeus! Adeus! Seria uma pena: a Maria Luísa tem uma pele que é um íman (um íman! Perfeita imagem!) e, não esqueçamos, na minha idade . . . (97)

> When it suits me, and if there were a motive (and if I were disposed to heed the motive, of course), I'd kick out my third wife and goodbye to her! Goodbye! It would be a shame: Maria Luísa has skin that is irresistible (like a magnet! A perfect image!). And let's not forget, at my age . . .

While Carlos does not get rid of Luísa, he nevertheless subjects her to a series of degrading situations. For example, in a conversation with Gil, who has been unable to find a woman who speaks English in order to entertain their client, Mr. Richardson, Carlos says: "—Tenho uma ideia . . . uma ideia estonteante: leve a Maria Luísa. O Richardson há-de gostar" (46) (I have an idea . . . a fascinating idea: take Maria Luísa. Richardson would love it). Carlos' joking words suggest that, like Gil, he views Luísa as an object which, when no longer of interest, can be passed on (if only temporarily) to another man. Moreover, he says this in Luísa's presence, not only insulting her but giving her another subtle indication of her inability to keep him sufficiently satisfied and entertained.

If Gil and Carlos view Luísa as an object, Luísa is taught by society to see herself in similar terms. Consequently, she scrutinizes herself even more closely than the men around her in order to assure herself that she will appeal to them. In the subsequent passage, Luísa assumes the dual role of spectator and spectacle as she prepares herself to meet Carlos and Gil for lunch:

> O espelho reflecte-me. E eu digo à minha imagem: isso mesmo, Luisinha, tira o casaco, ficas mais bela assim, a combinação lilás deixa entrever os teus encantos, e os teus encantos—não o negues, Luisinha! —constituem o mais poderoso dos teus credores. (54)

> The mirror reflects me. And I say to my image: that's right, Luisinha, take off your jacket, you look more beautiful that way. The lilac-colored slip subtly discloses your charms, and—don't deny it, Luisinha—you are powerfully indebted to your charms.

As a statement of a woman's oppression and confinement, this moment in her room is one of the most powerful and suggestive in the book. As she enters her bedroom, she throws a magazine on the bed, which she ironically refers to as the "cama-sarcófago" (bed-sarcophagus). The term is appropriate in the sense that it reflects her perception of the state of her "dying" marriage which, in turn, influences profoundly her diminishing sense of self. As Luísa turns to the mirror, she sees herself not in relief, but as an object among the many other objects in the room:

> A posição do espelho com moldura doirada (também doirada!) permite-me que nele me veja, como vejo o estofo adamascado dum cadeirão, a coluna de três pernas, o *teddy-bear* de peluche ... tudo enquadrado pelos limites da moldura como numa cela, sob o frontão, também doirado (um frontão que me pesa, uma coisa horrível!), com rosas e folhas bem sólidas, grossas como punhos, entrechocando as respectivas forças, comendo-se mutuamente os relevos, amigavelmente se encaixando e em parte se eliminando. (53–54)

> The position of the mirror with the golden frame (also golden!) lets me see myself in it, as I see the damask fabric of a large chair, the column with three feet, the plush teddy bear ... everything fitting within the borders of the frame as in a cell, under the frontal piece, also golden (a frontal piece that weighs me down, a horrid thing!) with roses and leaves solid and large like fists, their respective forces colliding, their reliefs mutually eating one another up, amicably encasing one another and in part eliminating one another.

The framed mirror also suggests her confinement. The heavy, ornate *frontão* or frontal piece, which is superimposed and crowns this reflection, reinforces the image of imprisonment; the large roses and leaves adorning the piece, which appear "like fists" pushing against one another, evoke images of beauty and self-destruction, both of which are symbols of her condition as a woman.

Luísa's escape from her "cell" and from her husband occurs later that same day. After spending the night on the town, Gil takes the drunken Luísa to her aunt's house, where Vina and Berto have been anxiously awaiting news of her. Fearful that Carlos will not take Luísa back, Tia Vina beseeches Berto to call Carlos and tell him that Luísa had returned hours ago, but that she has been ill. Berto reluctantly agrees to telephone Carlos with this story, and shortly thereafter Carlos appears to take Luísa home. The final scene shows all five characters together for the first time in the book. Luísa's "escape" has put all the others into action, since, for most of her life, she has depended upon them for support or assistance. In fact, up to this point, Luísa has viewed her life exclusively in terms of the actions of others. For example, the death of her aunt's benefactor, the Condessa, resulted in her being brought to Lisbon to live with her aunt and be educated; her relationship with Gil ended with his presenting her to Carlos; Cristina's rejection of Carlos brought about her marriage to Carlos; and now Tia Vina and Berto conspire to get Carlos to take her back.

But Luísa's submissiveness and her willingness to let others live her life come to an abrupt halt in the final scene. For the first time, Luísa rejects the help of others, and she confronts her husband with the truth: that she was drunk and stayed out the entire evening until the early hours of the morning. At this point, the ironic relationship between Luísa and Scheherazade becomes more explicit, more clearly related to the theme of fiction and survival. Carlos' response to Luísa's statement subtly reaffirms her feeling that her whole life has been a kind of lie (or a fiction), for he says she must believe in what others have said and have done to protect her for her own well-being, even if it is not based on truth:

—Ouve-me, Luísa: eu sei que ele [Berto] mentiu. Nem por um instante acreditei no que ele disse. Mas é como se acreditasse, e é

preciso que se passe o mesmo contigo. É preciso que ambos
acreditemos. Será a tua cura. (268)

"Listen to me Luísa: I know he [Berto] lied. Not for a single instant
did I believe in what he said. But I pretended to believe and you must
do the same. It's necessary that we both believe. It will be your cure."

That Luísa refuses to "entertain" her husband with the invented story
of her illness suggests her attempt to break with the Scheherazade role
created for her. Because she no longer feels the need to perform for
Carlos, she refuses to tell him a story and confronts him with the
truth. Furthermore, she implies that everything she has said in order
to please him has been based on untruths:

—Tu és feliz, Luísa. Tu és feliz comigo. Porque desistir?
—Eu contei que era feliz, não sei a quem, mas contei. (268)

"You are happy, Luísa. You are happy with me. Why give up?"
"I told someone I was happy, I don't remember who, but that's what I
told them."

The repetition of the word *contar* (to tell) in her response emphasizes the fact that Luísa has basically sacrificed her well-being in
order to "tell" others what they wanted to hear. Her resolve not to
tell another story is an indication of her desire to stop relying upon
the will of others to dictate her course in life, as well as an acknowledgement that she can no longer abide by the rules laid down for
women, rules that force them to perform (or to tell stories) in order
to keep men amused.

Of course, in one sense, Luísa can never stop telling stories, nor can
she escape the prison-house of language. After all, the "self" is always
a fiction, a necessary fabrication we make in order to live in society. It
is not clear whether Botelho recognizes that fact, and, as previously
indicated, her reliance on the paraphernalia of myth and classical
tragedy means that in certain ways she is still using a discourse inherited from a male-dominated literary tradition. At least, however, she
shows us that Luísa need not stop speaking altogether, and that her
storytelling might one day assume a different form. Indeed, Botelho's
own experimental technique, which problematizes the role of an

authorial voice in fiction, suggests that she herself feels constrained by her role. As a woman writer in the years of a fascist dictatorship, she hints that her own performance can be viewed ironically; her sudden appearance as "author" in the section entitled "Coro II" reveals that at some level she is caught up in the process she describes and perhaps wants to break free of it.

In this regard, it is important to emphasize that even though *Xerazade e os Outros* is subtitled a "tragedy," it does not end on a desperate note like Chopin's *The Awakening*. Botelho skillfully avoids a strong closure by having Luísa utter the ambiguous words "bom dia" (good morning), leaving the reader without a clear sense of what will happen afterward. The book's somewhat open ending points to the fact that the social conditions it describes will go on, involving a further struggle to make new and more liberating fictions of the self. Only a decade later, that struggle would move to the forefront of Portuguese literature, in ways Botelho had never expected.

NOTES

1. Born in Porto in 1926, Botelho was a student of classical philology at the universities of Coimbra and Lisbon and, like many young writers of the postwar period, she began her literary career by collaborating on journals and reviews dedicated to experimental writing. More than two dozen of these avant-garde, small press publications circulated during the fifties; although most were short lived, together they formed a distinctive voice which, in opposition to the entrenched neorealist movement, heralded the advent of existentialism and a neometaphysical poetry in Portugal. One of the more prominent journals of this group, *Távola Redonda*, published Botelho's book of poems, *As Coordenadas Líricas* (The Lyrical Coordinates); her novella, *O Enigma das Sete Alíneas* (The Enigma of the Seven Lines), was featured in the first issue of *Graal*, another popular vanguard publication. In quick succession, Botelho authored *O Angulo Raso* (The Level Angle) (1957), *Calendário Privado* (Private Calendar) (1958), and *A Gata e a Fábula* (The Cat and the Fable (1960), which was awarded the Prêmio Camilo Castelo Branco, one of the country's most prestigious literary prizes. Botelho published two novels shortly after *Xerazade e os Outros*: *Terra Sem Música* (Land without Music) (1969) and *Lourenço é Nome de Jogral* (Lourenço Is a Minstrel's Name) (1971). In 1987, the editorial firm Contexto, which is currently reprinting all

of her novels, published her new book entitled *Esta Noite Sonhei com Brueghel* (Tonight I Dreamed of Brueghel).

Most of the bibliography on Botelho is concerned primarily with her fourth novel, *Xerazade e os Outros*. See, for example, Fernando Mendonça, "As Relações Humanas e os Mitos da Profundidade" (Human Relations and the Myths of Profundity) (1966) and "Ficção de Autoria Feminina ou o Sabor da Solidão" (Fiction of Female Authorship or the Style of Solitude) (1973); Manuel Poppe, "Literatura e o Absurdo—*Xerazade e os Outros*" (Literature and the Absurd—*Xerazade e os Outros*) (1982); Maria Aparecida Ribeiro, "A Origem da Estrutura Trágica de *Xerazade e os Outros* (Origin of the Tragic Structure in *Xerazade e os Outros*) (1977); and Maria da Glória Martins Rebelo, "Fernanda Botelho: A Literatura como Matéria Romanesca" (Fernanda Botelho: Literature as Romanesque Material) (11 March, 25 March 1978). One of the best articles on *Xerazade e os Outros* can be found in José Palla e Carmo's collection of essays, *Do Livro à Leitura: Ensaios de Crítica Literária* (From Text to Reading: Essays of Literary Criticism) (1971).

2. See, for example, Raymond Williams' account of modernist drama in his book *Culture* (1981), pp. 172–80.

3. In his essay "Literatura e 'literariedade': '*Xerazade e os Outros*' de Fernanda Botelho," (Literature and "literarity": Fernanda Botelho's *Xerazade e os Outros*) José Palla e Carmo calls attention to this interesting correspondence between parts 1 and 2. See his *Do Livro à Leitura* (1971), p. 128.

4. One might say that the "Coro II" is modeled after the *parabasis* in Greek Old Comedy. Here, the chorus turns to the audience and speaks to them directly on behalf of the author, interpreting his point of view, expressing his concerns about writing, and even commenting on his real-life problems.

III

REVOLUTION AND REPRESENTATION IN LÍDIA JORGE'S O DIA DOS PRODÍGIOS

Among the new generation of writers to emerge in Portugal since 1974, one of the most innovative and important figures is the novelist Lídia Jorge. Her first book, *O Dia dos Prodígios* (The Day of Wonders) (1980), already recognized by the literary press in her own country as a masterpiece, deserves closer scrutiny and much wider attention.[1] The value of this work lies partly in its treatment of heretofore neglected problems in the Portuguese national life, and partly in its implicit demonstration of a close relationship between form and ideology. Throughout the novel—which attempts to describe how a relatively primitive section of the culture responds to modernity and revolution—Jorge has relied upon a series of unusual representational techniques, some of which are different from anything in the best-known contemporary fiction. She writes about a period of major political change, and in raising questions about the efficacy and direction of that change, she seems to feel a need to reshape novelistic conventions at basic levels.

In a lecture presented at the Universidade de Lisboa in March 1986, Jorge commented on the importance of the Portuguese revolution to her book, describing the novel as a metaphor for April 25, 1974—an historic date, now a national holiday, which took the peo-

ple by surprise and promised them a better future. But the novel por-
trays the memorable day in terms of a village community for whom the
revolution has no meaning. Their disillusionment and confusion following their brief encounter with strange, godlike soldiers can be understood in broader terms as an attempt to represent the attitude of
the entire nation, who believed the revolution would bring an end to
all their problems. Jorge's title for the book is therefore an ironic commentary on April 25, in that "the day of wonders" has come and gone,
without fulfilling everyone's expectations.

The formal irony of *O Dia dos Prodígios* and its power as a social
metaphor are due in large part to its unorthodox setting. Somewhat
like William Faulkner in America, Jorge devotes her book to a sparsely
populated, virtually ignored part of the nation—her birthplace, the
southern Algarve.[2] Although the coastal regions of this province are
celebrated internationally as a fashionable resort and vacation area,
inland lies a rural community unknown to and untouched by the industrial age. Cut off from the rest of Portugal by the Monchique and
Caldeirão mountain ranges to the north and removed from the relatively cosmopolitan centers like Faro and Albufeira that dot the coast,
the Algarvian community of the interior constitutes a displaced Third
World, totally dependent on its own meager resources for survival.
Jorge's novel creates a fictional version of that world, and by means of
a technique that is sometimes reminiscent of an older, oral tradition,
it depicts the reactions of the villagers as they come in contact with a
twentieth-century social revolution.

By making her protagonist a preindustrial community, Jorge implicitly rejects or ignores one of the chief concerns of Western fiction
from the eighteenth century onward: the growth (or decline) of the
individual in bourgeois capitalist society. In this respect and in others,
her text has a certain "folklorist" quality. Even though she is writing
about one of the most tradition-bound areas of the country, she also
wants to deal both sympathetically and critically with the Portuguese
revolution, suggesting certain problems the nation as a whole faces as
it enters the mainstream of European history. Jorge's audience, after
all, is not the Algarvian peasantry but the literate contemporary public in the cities. She writes as if she wanted to address that audience in
relatively baffling terms—defamiliarizing the narrative, showing the
impact of the revolution on the mind of the rural Algarve, and forcing

her most sophisticated readers out of complacent assumptions or typical habits of understanding.

Certain fantastic elements in Jorge's plot create an effect similar to Latin American fiction during the late 1960s and 1970s, when writers frequently used fables and the supernatural in their stories about underdeveloped communities. We should not be surprised at this affinity, since the form that came to be known as "magical realism" was an attempt by writers from Third World countries to evoke an experience outside modern rationalism, impinged upon by contemporary history. Jorge has similar ends in mind, and to some extent she could be said to participate in a general movement; her fictional Algarvian village, named Vilamaninhos, seems rather like a European variant of Juan Rulfo's Comala and Gabriel García Márquez's Macondo. But a remote agrarian setting and supernaturally motivated events are only isolated aspects of her novel, and she cannot be easily compartmentalized. Like some magical realists, Jorge is a politically engaged writer who is sympathetic with revolutionary change; at the same time, she is skeptical of utopian politics and somewhat disenchanted with recent history. Her attitude—both toward the Algarve culture and toward the revolutionary soldiers—is complex, a commingling of satire and respect. As if to reflect this position, the novel itself is a finely balanced mixture of the radically old and the radically new; a folkloric tale that is also an ironic, decentered text, it occasionally employs a special typography to signify its difference from ordinary fiction. Ultimately, we might describe it as an attempt to forge a new consciousness, dependent on a synthesis of preindustrial storytelling and experimental techniques—a strategy that leads Jorge to the abandonment of a purely realistic sense of probability and a highly unusual way of depicting speech or voice on the page.[3]

Before discussing the formal and ideological implications of O Dia dos Prodígios in further detail, it may be useful to comment on certain events in the book, noting how Jorge blends fantasy with documentary detail, legend with contemporary politics, and wonder with irony. The novel concerns slightly more than a year in the life of its fictional village, but a significant digression near the beginning tells us something about the history of the place. It seems Vilamaninhos was founded by the ancestors of one of its oldest inhabitants, José Jorge Júnior. According to this eccentric fellow, whose two principal activities are lifting heavy chairs with one hand and recalling the past, the founders initially lived in Vilamurada, a nearby settlement once re-nowned for its rich farming lands. Strategically located on the banks of the river, Vilamurada was frequently pillaged by the king's soldiers, who would pass by the village on their way south to the coastal centers of Faro and Tavira. Tired of the soldiers' lootings, the villagers, under the leadership of José Jorge, the great-great-great-great-grandfather of José Jorge Júnior, left and resettled in a less fertile area which they named Vilamaninhos. There, for many years, they passed a relatively quiet existence, until one day a soldier appeared, looking for José Jorge.

The founding of communities without a royal charter was a punish-able act, and the soldier had come on behalf of the king to collect for the crime. José Jorge, now an old man, rose out of his chair and shouted at the soldier, saying that he knew of no such king. He further challenged the royal messenger's authority by telling him that if the king did exist, he should stick to ruling his own lands. As the ultimate act of defiance, the old man turned his back on the soldier, dropped his pants, and bent over as far as his frail body would allow him to go. In response, the indignant soldier got off his horse, grabbed a pig from a nearby herd, and rode off with it squealing and defecating under his arm. In José Jorge Júnior's words, it was a day never to be forgotten; not long after, the river feeding their land went dry, and the villagers have been waiting for the waters to return ever since.

This small, almost self-contained episode from the early history of Vilamaninhos reveals three important qualities of Jorge's book as a whole. First of all, it is delivered to us as a tale passed down from gen-eration to generation—a carnivalistic, narrated story which does not render the action through dialogue or any of the psychological para-phernalia of a realist novel. Its slightly comic, folkloric tone is en-hanced by a second important quality: in the world of Vilamaninhos, nature is an active character, responding directly to events in "magi-cal" ways. A river dries up in response to the old man's defiance—an event which is presented quite matter-of-factly, as if the natural world were not separate or "other" but possessed of a volitional drive similar to human beings. Finally, the story tells us something important about the relation of the village to the rest of the country. It should be recalled that Portugal was ruled by a monarchy for over 700 years until the republic was proclaimed in 1910. That the people of Vila-maninhos have no notion of the monarchy and even challenge its authority suggests the extent to which they are removed from the national life.

As we learn subsequently, things have not really changed: like their forefathers, the current residents have either no knowledge or only a vague idea of what is happening outside. Everywhere in the novel, history has been absorbed into folklore, and it is represented obliquely or ironically. This fact is made quite clear near the middle of the book, when Jorge introduces a significant allusion to the nation as a whole. After Portugal has been engaged in more than ten years of fighting, the village finally learns that a colonial war is going on in Africa. Until this point, the reader has no notion that the action of *O Dia dos Prodígios* is taking place in a contemporary, datable frame of time (1973 to 1974). Jorge has purposely kept us in a state somewhat analogous to that of the majority of the villagers, who have no knowledge of current national events. But unlike the villagers, we bring to the book a sense of modern history, and once "outside" information is introduced, the whole status of the novel undergoes a basic change. Now the text is no longer a modern approximation of a faraway, rather exotic community; as privileged onlookers, we recognize that contemporary life has ruptured the folkloric world.

The villagers are spellbound by historical events, and yet the subsequent news of the revolution, like that of the war, seems to have no real consequence for them. Because they have so little inkling of what is happening in the country, they perceive the revolution not as a new political order announcing the end of a fascist regime, but as a miracle performed by supernatural beings who are going to bring some undefined change. For this reason, the community simply marvels at what the arriving soldiers look like; the villagers hope to communicate with the outsiders, but they have no way of measuring or comprehending a new, predemocratic form of government. In fact, Vilamaninhos has a history of its own, responsive to the seasons and quite free of the timesense of the modern consciousness. More central to the village than national wars or revolution is an entirely local incident which occurs at the outset of the book, an incident that draws the community together in fear and expectation of some radical change to come. A snake slithers into the center of the village and frightens some children, who try but fail to kill it. Their cries for help are answered by Jesuína Palha, a robust peasant woman, who, like a female St. George, launches into a long and difficult battle with the creature to save the community from evil. A powerful stench fills the air as Jesuína's repeated blows crush the serpent, forcing its entrails to spill out on the road. A few of the bystanders, overwhelmed by the nauseating odor exuded by the snake, rush to the side of the road to vomit in the bushes. Having fought and won the battle, Jesuína refrains from beheading her victim and decides instead to hang its corpse in the boughs of a tree as a warning to other possible intruders. Just as she picks it up with a stick, displaying it on high for all to see, the serpent comes alive; writhing and hissing, sprouting iridescent wings, it takes flight and vanishes into thin air.

We do not witness this event as it occurs; rather, we learn of it from Jesuína and others, who rush to the house of Carma Rosa and her daughter, Carminha, to confront them with the details. These two are frequently sought out and blamed whenever anything unusual or bad happens in the village. Years ago, Carma had an affair with the former parish priest, who, learning that she was pregnant, disappeared from the village, leaving Carma and their child, Carminha, to face the wrath of the community alone. Scorned by most, the two women live quietly on the edge of the community and rarely leave their house to see what is going on. Indignant that Carma and Carminha were not there to witness the snake, Jesuína uses the episode as a means of chastising the women for their past sins and present indifference. In recounting the event, she implies that they are the ones responsible for the entire incident and for what she views as the curse put upon the whole village by the evil serpent.

This crucial episode, which begins the action of the novel, is not described as an hallucination, but as a fact. It is one of several fabulous or magical happenings which are treated as a natural part of day-to-day life, so that the entire world of the novel has the feel of myth. The book is filled with mock-epic or extraordinary characters and events; thus we meet Branca, a sort of village Penelope, who has spent the ten years of her marriage sewing a quilt, while her husband, José Pássaro Volante, rides his mule about the countryside trading and selling. At the beginning of the book we learn that Branca can hear sounds far off in the distance. Her hearing is so acute that she recognizes the braying of Pássaro's mule, who has run away into the backlands to escape mistreatment from his brutish master. Although Branca knows the mule's whereabouts, she conceals it from Pássaro, preferring that the mule wander freely rather than become, like her, a slave and victim of her husband's temperamental outbursts. As the novel progresses, Branca takes on other supernatural traits. She begins to sleep with her eyes open, and she can read people's thoughts. Her quilt also has strange powers. As she nears its completion, the dragon design in the center takes on a terrifying aspect, similar to the fiery, winged snake that appeared in the beginning of the book. Branca is at once captivated and fearful of her creation: the dragon seems to come alive as she works on it, becoming an entity whose powers are beyond comprehension and control. Perhaps the most astonishing thing about such episodes is that no one ever questions them. Branca's transformation from a submissive housewife to a visionary and oracle merely happens, and it is accepted by those around her as part of the ordinary course of events. Even Pássaro takes his wife's transformation in stride, despite the fact that by the end of the book, he is completely under her control.

Ultimately, however, strange occurrences like the flying snake are balanced with "realistic" but equally fabulous events from contemporary history. For example, the first sign of the colonial war in Africa comes with the arrival in the village of a young man whose attire immediately attracts attention. As he makes his way to Carma's house, one of the villagers, a veteran of the First World War, recognizes the outfit to be a uniform, and he informs the others that the fellow is a soldier. Just as the episode with the snake drew the community together in an attempt to decipher its significance, the soldier's arrival causes them to convene and speculate on his presence; in fact, he is so unusual that the villagers wonder whether he is some kind of divine messenger who has come to solve the mystery of the snake. Carma dispels this notion completely by informing them that he is her godchild and that he has come to court Carminha before going off to war. This announcement is doubly disconcerting to the villagers: not only does it dash their hopes for an answer to the riddle of the snake, it also confuses them, since they had no idea that a war was taking place.

After a brief courtship with Carminha, the soldier departs. Some time later, we learn indirectly of his death, in a passage remarkable for its satiric use of what Mikhail Bakhtin might have described as the "bodily lower stratum."[4] Carminha's mother rushes to an outhouse, clutching in her hand a piece of newspaper which she found wrapped around a bar of soap in the cupboard. As she relieves herself, she glances at the scrap of paper and sees in the bottom corner a box with a black border, a cross, and special lettering. The paper, we gradually realize, is a fragment from an old obituary page, which announces the death of Carminha's fiancé. Carma struggles to free herself from the outhouse and find her daughter, who stares at the notice in shock and disbelief. Not only has the death been discovered in a ludicrous fashion, but its ultimate tragedy is undermined: the obituary announces that, instead of dying in battle, the young man has accidentally shot and killed himself with his own gun.

An even more cynical view of the war, which appears in a later section of the book, has to do with Carminha's second fiancé, a sergeant who arrives mysteriously in the village and begins to court the young woman. Unlike the first soldier, the sergeant imposes himself on the community, using them as an audience for his tales about wartime Africa. He complains about the lack of food and the susceptibility to disease in Africa, and he criticizes the native culture. Central to his story is his chilling description of his participation in atrocities, such as the killing of a group of defenseless lepers and his bartering for the virgin daughter of a poor African family. Even more gruesome than these acts are the enthusiasm and the delight with which the sergeant recalls his adventures, abetted by an unnamed, fictional narrator who repeatedly alludes to the fact that we are hearing a "story," intended to entertain.

Eventually the village is visited by a whole group of soldiers, who have come to the countryside to inform the people of the revolution. The following description of the soldiers' entrance into Vilamaninhos is illustrative of the mystical effect that people and events from the outside have on the villagers' lives:

. . . O que vejo, meu deus? Vem aí um carro. Um carro celestial. Celestial. Olhem todos. Traz os anjos e os arcanjos. Oh gente. E São Vicente por piloto. Disse Jesuína Palha que voltava da ceifa, ainda com o avental e o lenço repletos de praganas. Todos olharam. Na verdade surgia na curva da estrada, pelo lado poente, qualquer coisa de tão extravagante que todos os que conseguiam enxergar a mancha de cores, virando as cabeças julgaram ir cair de borco sobre o chão da rua. . . . Mas os homens, pondo a mão, e fazendo muito esforço para verem claro o que avançava com tanta majestade, disseram. Menos rápidos e mais lúcidos. Vamos. Vamos ser visitados por seres saídos do céu, e vindos de outras esferas. Onde os séculos têm outra idade. Afastem-se, vizinhos, que esta visão costuma fulminar. (152)

. . . My god, what do I see? Here comes a car. A celestial car. Celestial. Look everybody. It's carrying angels and archangels. Oh, people. And St. Vincent is driving. Said Jesuína Palha, who was returning from the harvest with her apron and scarf still filled with awns. Everyone looked. In fact, at the bend in the road, on the side where the sun sets, there appeared a thing so utterly remarkable that those who managed to make out the spot of colors, turning their heads, thought they would fall face down on the ground in the road . . . . But the men, shading their eyes with their hands, and making every effort to see clearly what was approaching so majestically, said. Less rapidly and more lucidly. We're going. We're going to be visited by heavenly beings from other worlds. Where centuries have a different age. Get back neighbors, for this vision is likely to strike us down like lightning.

While the villagers respond favorably to the soldiers' flag-waving and slogans, they are confused by other aspects of the visit. For instance, when the soldiers inform them that the revolution was fought on behalf of the "humilhados e oprimidos" (humble and oppressed), the villagers ask, "Quem são esses?" (Who are those?) The soldiers' reply, "São vocês" (They are you), startles the villagers, since they have no conception of themselves as constituting a particular class, let alone an oppressed class for whom the revolution was fought. Furthermore, the soldiers act strangely when Jesuína asks them to explain the significance of the snake. Because they do not comprehend her request, Jesuína retells the story. Amused by the account, the soldiers respond by patronizing the villagers, telling them that it is gratifying to see a people who still believe in miracles.

The novel ends shortly after the soldiers' abrupt departure from the village. Despite the many "wonders" that have been encountered, no fundamental change has been wrought, and we have no sense that the narrative is moving toward a revelation of truth or a feeling of progress in the lives of the characters. Disillusioned by what they hoped would be the answer to their specific concerns, the villagers can only comfort one another by finding imaginative uses for the soldiers' visit. Sitting around and talking about this and other events, they add still another chapter to their storytelling existence.

The habit of telling stories seems central to the life of the village, and it affects the way in which Jorge renders events in the book. Throughout, she has abandoned the representational techniques of the realist social novel—partly because she wants to find a formal correlative for the experience of people in southern Portugal, partly because she rejects the ideology of mainstream industrial society. In effect, she wants not only to describe something different, but also to describe it in a radically different way, bringing the oldest "ways of seeing" into a modern era. The extent of her effort may not be apparent from the foregoing description, which concentrates mainly on the fantastic qualities of the novel's plot. The experience of reading *O Dia dos Prodígios*, however, involves the reader in other, perhaps more basic kinds of strangeness. Throughout, Jorge deploys an unorthodox language, often combining local dialect with formalized and lyric qualities; she also adopts a variety of unusual narrative techniques dependent on a peculiar typographic style.

There is insufficient space here to analyze all her devices, but one of them deserves special attention. Her most visibly striking departure from convention has to do with the way in which speech is represented, so that what is heard is not individuals engaged in conversations or in introspective musings, but a community telling stories or making public announcements. In this respect her writing stands in vivid contrast to what we commonly regard as novelistic discourse. For example, in ordinary realist fiction, when two or more characters speak, their words to one another are graphically separated on the page, and narrative cues or shifters enable the reader to identify the speaker at any given moment. Dialogue therefore becomes a fundamentally linear activity—a give-and-take of questions, responses, or interjections which mark time and signal cause and effect; set off in the text by some form of punctuation, it amounts to a special category of language, providing the reader with a sense of dramatic immediacy, individual subjectivity, and narrative development.[5] Jorge takes a different approach, challenging the romantic-realist conception of speech by suppressing it or representing it in quite indirect ways.

We can sense the implications of her method at the beginning of the novel in the episode with the snake. I quote a rather lengthy passage, beginning with a brief narrative introduction, to give a sense of the role graphic representation plays in the reformulation of speech:

Jesuína Palha. À frente. Galgava de três em três as lajes como se viesse cumprir uma missão de urgência. Atrás dela muitas sem lenço. . . . Em fileira miúda, rapazes e crianças vinham correndo lestos, acompanhando o passo da subida. Chegaram à porta em dois grupos. Como se fossem cercar a entrada. . . . E Jesuína Palha olhando-as nos olhos. Primeiro muda. Como se as ameaçasse, sem conseguir fazer uma palavra com a língua.

Ah filhas da su mãe. Que aqui estão estas duas dentro de casa sem saberem de coisíssima nenhuma. Não me digam que não ouviram um barulho de gente rebolvida. E estas aqui debaixo de telha e à fresca. Eu. Jesuína Palha. Eu andava a dar fogo ao forno quando ouvi estes três desgraçados a pedirem acuda. Mas não deixi que pedissem duas vezes. Pus os tojos de lado, salti por cima da parede, pegui uma cana comprida que ali tinha à mão, e fui-me para onde estes três vai não vai tentavam matá-la. Sem conseguirem os pobrezinhos. Ah meus amigos. Ah carago. Já a família desta terra estava chegando ao largo. Ali. Eles que digam. Estavam todos suadinhos de tanta pedrada sobre a magana. Ah meus amigos, vizinhos da minha alma. Quando vi a víbora cegui os olhos. Alavanti a saia, brandi a cana, uma, duas, três, sete e vinte vezes sobre a cabeça da bicha. . . . Di-lhe bem umas trinta canadas sobre a espinha e a cabeça. Di ou não di? E a língua dela, que parece uma gancha de cabelo, andava dentro e fora a desafiar a cana. E

Toda a gente vinha correndo a ver a cobra. Chegui eu nessa altura. E vinha tão cega, que nem me apercebi do que via.

A gente viu. Deu-lhe com a cana em cima e a valhaca esgueirava-se para a embeiradinha da berma. A vizinha com

ela à roda. À roda, à roda sem
parar. Toda a gente se tinha já
alevantado da cama. Das suas
mesas e outras dos lavadoiros
... (21–23)

o instrumento na mão, afegava
como se cavasse chão duro do
ter-reirão da rua.

Jesuína Palha. In the lead. Taking the steps three at a time as if she were
coming to carry out an urgent mission. Behind her were many without
scarves. . . . In a small row, young boys and little children came running
sprightly after them, up the steps. They arrived at the door in two
groups. As if they were about to surround the entrance. . . . And
Jesuína Palha looking them in the eye. Silent at first. As if she were
threatening them, without forming a single word with her tongue.

Oh bad seeds. Here these two
are at home not knowing a thing
that is going on. Don't tell me
you didn't hear the sound of
people in an uproar. And here
you are cool beneath your roof.
I. Jesuína Palha. I was making a
fire in the oven when I heard
these three poor creatures calling out for help. They didn't
have to call twice. I dropped the
kindling, jumped the wall,
picked up a long stick that was
near at hand, and I went to
where these three were trying to
kill it. Without succeeding, the
poor things. Oh my friends. Oh
shit. Everybody was already
coming into the square. There.
Let them tell you. Everyone was
soaked with sweat from having
thrown so many stones at the
rascal. Oh my friends, my dear-
est neighbors. When I saw the
snake, I was blinded. I picked up
my skirt, and lowered the stick,
one, two, three, seven, and
twenty times on the snake's
head. . . . I struck it a good

Everybody came running to see
the snake. I arrived just about
then. And I was so out of it
that I didn't realize what I was
seeing.

thirty times on its back and head. Did I or didn't I? And its tongue, looking like a long curl of hair, moving in and out, defying the stick. And it went around. Round and round, without stopping. Everybody had already got out of their beds or up from their tables. Others stopped in the middle of washing.

People saw. She struck it and the scoundrel tried to crawl toward the side of road. With the stick in her hand, our neighbor was panting as if digging solid ground in the public square.

This particular graphic rendition of speech appears just twice in the novel, once in the beginning and once in the end. Interestingly, in both instances the circumstances are largely the same. Jesuína, accompanied by members of the village, hurries to Carma's house to bring her and her daughter the news of some unforeseen event. The first event described is the appearance of the snake; the second is the discovery that a revolution has taken place. Thus, in addition to representing speech, the double column acts as a motif, signifying a momentous set of conditions.[6]

The organization of speech into two columns graphically imitates the simultaneous approach of two groups of individuals to Carma's door; furthermore, the blank spaces on the right serve to highlight Jesuína's public harangue, setting her words apart from a blankness or silence around them, which is occasionally broken by short statements from a crowd. Note, however, that while it is clear that Jesuína is the speaker on the left, the exact identity of the speaker or speakers on the right is never revealed. The use of phrases such as "toda a gente" (everyone) and "a gente" (the people) and, in later passages, the appearance of first-person plural verb forms such as *pressentíamos* (we sensed) and *víamos* (we saw) suggest that what we are hearing on the right is a communal voice—an "I" who could be everyone and nobody in particular, representing bystanders who simply confirm Jesuína's epic tale. Everywhere, in fact, the rather formalized repetitions and other similarities in the two columns tend to emphasize the collective nature of the experience.

As mentioned earlier, speech in conventional novels is represented as a linear activity: although a certain degree of naturalistic overlapping can be indicated in passages of dialogue, one character's words follow another's on the page—an order which both preserves identity and helps to forward the narrative. Unlike most novelists, however, Jorge is not interested in depicting the give-and-take of individual voices, nor in most of the conventions we usually accept as lifelike; instead, she develops an alternative form, often suggesting many people speaking about the same subject at the same point in time. There is a somewhat disorienting quality to this technique: not only do the comments overlap completely, but they also tend toward a kind of redundancy. Unlike the conventional linear style, the double column forces the reader to cross back and forth from one discourse to another, much in the same way a listener in a crowd must transfer his or her attention to one, then another speaker. But the exact temporal relation between the two columns is not always clear. In some cases, the reader is required to forsake any expectation that speech will be a chronological and individualized act; the text becomes relatively polyphonic, decentered, and nonlinear.

What is equally interesting about the double column is the unusual mode of address used by the characters, one which evokes an older, oral form of literature. For example, the passage cited above focuses on a confrontation between Jesuína and the mother and daughter; ironically, however, neither Carma nor her daughter respond to Jesuína's accusations and insults. The only other voice in the narrative is that of the villagers, who intermittently confirm and elaborate what Jesuína says. The same thing happens in the scene at the end of the book, where the double column form reappears. Jesuína describes the wonders of the revolution and accuses Carma and her daughter of being indifferent, while they remain perfectly silent. In both instances Jorge employs a mode of speaking that is radically different from dramatic exchange in conventional novels. Indeed, if we study the book closely, we find that Jorge's characters rarely speak with the intent of eliciting a response. As the passage above illustrates, their words to one another have a rhetorical, *presentational* quality; they are filled with diction and expressions specific to the oral culture of the Algarve, but they are spoken as if from a podium.[7]

A great many of the standard conventions of dramatic discourse in fiction were of course developed out of the culture of an industrialized middle class; to Jorge, they seem inappropriate for a book about a community which is not far removed from the feudal past. In their place, she has developed a highly stylized form—an "epic" address which conveys the feel of a centuries-old tradition of telling stories. Her double column technique is only one manifestation of this rhetoric. Consider, for example, another episode from early in the novel, which involves José Jorge Júnior and his wife, Esperança Teresa. An older couple, they stay mostly indoors and occasionally speak to one another as if to reaffirm their existence. In the following scene, José calls to his wife to join him at the table so she can better hear what he has to say:

> — ... Oh Esperancinha. O avô do avô desse meu avô, que comigo andou ao colo, nasceu das ervinhas. Encontraram-no dentro dum balaio como se fosse uma mão cheia de figos para dar a porcos. Ali no Vale Mortal no meio das mariolas e dos troviscos. Uma velha muita velha, mais velha que saragoça, oh Esperancinha. ...
> José Jorge Júnior sabe que sua mulher pode não o ouvir, mas sempre o escuta. E por isso chega-se mais junto dela, arrastando o banco para aí se empoleirar de novo. ...
> —A velha ao tempo já era bisavó duma porção de bisnetos, oh Esperancinha. ... Trouxe-o para casa, deu-lhe leite da cabra, papa de milho, umas colheres de batata doce, e não é que o raio desse meu avô começou a fazer-se gordinho, a crescer, a crescer e a medrar como se mamasse da mãe?
> —E eu doze vezes di à luz, José. Tu te alembras? Doze vezes. Primeiro foi o Manuel. Depois veio a Engrácia. Depois o Saul, depois o Elói. Depois o Bento. Depois o Augusto.
> —Tão gordinho, alto e espadaúdo, que apenas com quinze anos, Esperancinha, acabou por se chamar José Jorge. ... E assim José Jorge cresceu, ajuntou-se e gerou a Manuel Jorge. E Manuel Jorge gerou a José Jorge. E José Jorge a Manuel Jorge que foi meu avô, e meu avô. ...
> —Depois do Augusto julgui não poder conceber. Mas eram coisas passadoiras. Mistérios da barriga. Um dia fiquei do António. Depois do Marçal, e do Duarte. E do Simão. Depois o morto. (29–31)

"... Oh Esperancinha. The grandfather of my great-great-grandfather, who carried me in his arms, was an abandoned child. They found him in a small basket as if he

were a handful of figs to give to the pigs. There in Mortal
Valley in the midst of the mountains and the thunder. An
old woman, older than Saragossa, oh Esperancinha . . ."
José Jorge Júnior knows his wife might not hear him but always listens.
And therefore he moves closer to her, dragging the bench so he can sit on
it again. . . .
"At the time the old woman was already the great grand-
mother of a bunch of great grandchildren, oh Esperancinha. . . . She brought him home, gave him goat's milk,
corn gruel, and some spoonfuls of sweet potato, and
wouldn't you know, that rascal, my grandfather, started
getting fat, and began to grow, and grow, and bloom as if
nursed by his own mother."
"And I gave birth twelve times, José. Do you remember?
Twelve times. First there was Manuel. Then came
Engrácia. After that, Saul, then Elói. Then Bento. And
after him, Augusto."
"So fat, tall, and broad-shouldered, that when he was just fif-
teen, Esperancinha, he ended up being called José Jorge. . . .
And so José Jorge grew up, got a woman, and begat Manuel
Jorge. And Manuel Jorge begat José Jorge. And José Jorge
begat Manuel Jorge who was my grandfather. . . ."
"After Augusto I didn't think I could conceive anymore.
But all that passed. Mysteries of the womb. One day I got
with António. Then Marçal, and later Duarte. Then
Simão. Then the one who died."

In this passage, Jorge's technique seems slightly more conventional.
She uses a dash to introduce and distinguish the different characters'
words, and she alternates their respective speeches in a give-and-take
fashion. Although the graphic device which enables us to distinguish
a narrator from the characters is relatively unorthodox, it serves the
same function as paragraphing in ordinary prose. Nevertheless,
Jorge's apparently minor alteration of an otherwise traditional looking
format serves to call attention to the more unusual features of the
scene. Two characters are talking to one another across a table, but
even though José feels his wife "always listens," they are not engaged
in what we would normally call a conversation. Although the form
suggests a give-and-take, the individual speeches reveal that the characters are not responding to one another at all. Both talk about the
past, but they are reminiscing about different experiences. Caught up

in the world of his ancestors, José Jorge Júnior recalls the proud, patriarchal history of the family name, passed down in biblical fashion from father to son through successive generations. Absorbed in the more recent, maternal past, Esperança talks about the history of her own family and recites a similar sort of litany.

Ironically, this more traditional looking graphic representation of speech involves a more radical departure from conventional dramatic discourse than the double column form. In one sense, the double column is closer to realistic speech because what Jesuína and the villagers say is motivated by an external event—the appearance of a flying snake; Jesuína is in fact delivering a public oration, meant to impress the village, and like characters in a traditional novel, Carma and her daughter are portrayed as heeding what is ostensibly addressed to them. In the more conventional looking passage, on the other hand, there is no relationship between what the characters are talking about and what is happening at that particular moment—no sense that words are rising out of a circumstantial context. José and Esperança's words to one another concern private, abstract realities miraculously conjured up by the mere action of their sitting down at the table. There is no one present in the scene to hear their rhetorical, stylized remarks, and the husband and wife are so wrapped up in their individual reminiscings that neither seems to listen to what the other is saying.

This scene with José and Esperança might be understood as merely an attempt by the author to describe a situation in which two people, living together over a long period of time, no longer communicate. Neither is especially concerned with what the other has to say, and therefore they ramble on, unaware that they are talking about different things. But this interpretation seems inadequate, largely because the husband and wife are not talking about everyday concerns or private fears and frustrations. Rather, they are speaking about matters of generalized, historical importance. In a sense, Jorge is utilizing a dramatic setting—two people sitting down at a table—as a pretext for a more formal kind of discourse. Like figures in a tableau, each character is speaking a quasi-epic as opposed to a "realistic" language. José Jorge Júnior provides a stereotypical male history, whereas Esperança focuses on conception and the physical and psychological hardships women endure in their biological role as mothers; paralleled and contrasted over a space of five pages, their speeches represent an archetypal male and female discourse aimed *outward* toward the reader.

It is important to note that this particular form of address is used to record the speech of characters in a domestic situation. All of the exchanges in José Jorge Júnior and Esperança's home take this form. Although the technique is used primarily to record the words of the husband and wife, it is also used at times when a third party momentarily enters their home. For example, at one point in the novel, a neighbor, Maria Rebola, rushes into their house to describe the visit of the revolutionary soldiers. First Maria and José talk, later, Maria and Esperança speak. Once again, however, the characters do not seem to be engaged in a conversation. Maria's description of the visit is alternated first with José's, then with Esperança's ruminations about experiences related to the past. The episode is more realistic looking, largely because Maria's comments are motivated by an event in the plot—the soldiers' visit—and because, in describing the episode, she tries to impress upon the other two its significance. In the final analysis, however, both scenes involve a presentational form of address, in which characters seem to be *telling* rather than experiencing events.

Jorge achieves this sense of a community given over to oratory by engaging her characters in clearly rhetorical types of discussion and by interpolated commentaries identified in the text as "stories." The chief example of this technique is the sergeant's story based on his experiences in wartime Africa. The sergeant's tale, which extends over four pages, is frequently interrupted by an anonymous narrator, who gives an account of what is happening in the village as the story is being told. There are seven interruptions altogether, so that the reader is transported back and forth between descriptions of two very different worlds: Africa, where people are abused and murdered every day, and Vilamaninhos, whose daily events consist of such things as girls picking flowers and dogs copulating in the street. Paralleling and contrasting with the wartime account, the intervening commentary on the village slows down the pace of what the soldier is describing, making it seem like an extended, heroic adventure; the narrator also tends to reaffirm the fact that the sergeant is telling a story, and keeps the reader informed of its progress with statements like: "e o conto ia e vinha" (and the story came and went) and "de novo o conto vinha" (once again the story came). Hence the episode takes on a special significance in terms of the rhetorical strategy of the novel as a whole: not only does it portray an individual embellishing a tale, it also includes a fictional narrator who is a kind of second-level storyteller, adding references to the elaborate spinning of yarns.

This "rhetorical" feel of the novel is especially evident in scenes like the following, which document the community's reaction to a particular event. Here the villagers have gathered together to talk about their lives before and after the appearance of the snake:

> Manuel Gertrudes disse. Antes o arreeiro trazia outro peixe. E o arreeiro disse. Antes toda a gente só falava da frescura dele. E dava gosto vendê-lo. Jesuína Palha disse. Antes, mesmo em Agosto, não me fazia impressão o lenço. E Matilde disse. Antes bebia-se mais Lagoa, porque nesta venda falava-se de coisas simples. E Macário disse. Agora pouco se interessam pelo meu bandolim. Parece que andam a ouvir outra música. Manuel Gertrudes disse. Agora, vizinhança, estamos definitivamente longe da primeira guerra mundial. E João Martins disse. (43)

> Manuel Gertrudes said. Before the muleteer brought another kind of fish. And the muleteer said. Before everybody only talked about its freshness. And it was a pleasure to sell it. Jesuína Palha said. Before, even in August, my scarf didn't make a mark on me. And Matilde said. Before everybody was drinking more Lagoa, because they used to talk about simple things in this store. And Macário said. Now people are barely interested in my mandolin. It seems they are listening to another kind of music. Manuel Gertrudes said. Now, neighbors, we are definitely far from the First World War. And João Martins said.

Passages like this one appear throughout the book. Presentational in form, they function somewhat like a chorus in classical theater, commenting on the action. The importance of this particular device in the overall design of the novel is alluded to in a curious passage, structured much like the one above, which prefaces the book. Set apart from the rest of the text, which it categorizes as "uma história," it calls attention to the fact that a story is about to be told. It also suggests that what is about to follow is not a conventional narrative told by an individual or by a group speaking with a single voice. Rather, it is to be a story based on the observations of a group, members of which will somewhat ritualistically take turns speaking.

The passage cited above is representative of this collective commentary. Like verses in a poem, the alternating short and long sentences have a cadence, and a kind of internal rhyme is produced by the repetition of certain key words. The language of the villagers is therefore a special discourse, bordering on oral poetry and epic narration, directed toward a listener who seems more like an audience than like an interlocutor. By such means Jorge attempts to link Portugal's ancient village culture to its postrevolutionary future.

It now seems important to return to the problem of how Portuguese history helped to determine the form of the novel. In the most general sense, it seems clear that Jorge's antirealist plot and her unorthodox narrative technique are designed to convey a complex attitude toward Portugal's national culture. Long isolated from Europe and the rest of the world by a dictatorship and by an almost feudal provincial life, the country is now attempting to create a new society. Its problem, Jorge suggests, is to produce valid change, appropriate to the sense of "wonder" which accompanied the overthrow of the Salazar-Caetano regime. At the same time, modernity needs to be viewed with a healthy skepticism, so that Portugal will not be utterly absorbed by Western commercialism. This delicate process of change and social analysis is made all the more difficult because of differences among areas of the country, and because political divisions within the new democracy have tended to slow or deflect the original thrust of revolution.

Portugal's political situation in the aftermath of the revolution might be regarded as the "structuring absence" of Jorge's story. Indirectly, the novel reminds us that the overthrow of the fascist regime was carried out by the military, not by the nation as a whole. The entire course of the country was changed in a single day with an almost bloodless coup that shocked most of the population as well as every foreign government in the world. (To sense how little was known about the takeover at the time, we need only recall that the right-wing military governments of Brazil and Spain publicly saluted the revolution and that South Africa, unaware that decolonization was imminent, was among the first to recognize officially the new leadership [Gallagher 1983, 191].) Although most of the activities culminating in the revolution took place in Lisbon, all the major cities in Portugal joined the capital in celebrating the event; people flocked to the streets, dancing and singing, and they adorned the soldiers passing by in trucks and tanks with red carnations, which became a national symbol. It was not until some time later that the news of the revolution reached the outlying areas, especially the extreme north and south. Ironically, the reaction of people in those areas was a strange mixture of curiosity and disinterest, based on what they viewed as a bizarre yet meaningless event. Hence, the main task of the revolutionary soldiers traveling from village to village was to educate the inhabitants and to bring them into the twentieth century. But instead of drawing villagers closer to the modern age, the revolutionary teachings, which focused on such issues as birth control and anticlericalism, shocked the provincials to such a degree that they retreated even further into their highly traditional ways. Some reacted more strongly than others to what the soldiers said and did on their "cultural dynamizing" campaigns. For example, in the area of Tomar, in central Portugal, the villagers, preferring to be left alone than to submit to what they viewed as the heresies of modern living, stoned the soldiers (Gallagher 1983, 206).

It should be pointed out that Jorge's sympathy with the village's point of view is not a sign of a reactionary nostalgia. Her satiric treatment of the African war is one indication of her progressive politics, and in her public life she has repeatedly aligned herself with socialist reform. Moreover, her satire of the revolution's utopian qualities should not blind us to several facts: since the revolution, Portugal has liberated the colonies in Africa; has accommodated more than 650,000 *retornados* (returnees) resulting from the decolonization process; has drawn up a new constitution; has instituted free elections for national and local government officials; and has passed important social and economic legislation which introduced, among other things, social pensions, unemployment benefits, maternity provisions, and a national minimum wage (Balsemão 1986, 197; Robinson 1979, 261). These monumental achievements have been matched, however, by equally serious problems, all of which have an indirect bearing on Jorge's somewhat ironic novel. For example, the electoral system adopted in 1975 and written into the 1976 constitution makes it extremely difficult for any one of the four main political parties to win a majority of the votes (Bruneau and Macleod 1986, 30-31). As the historian Kenneth Maxwell pointed out in the mid-1980s:

Since 1974, there have been a total of 16 governments. Almost all have been marked by internal bickering and political paralysis . . . . Unlike Spain, for instance, where governments were able to function with solid parliamentary support either by agreements or by gaining clear elec-

toral majorities, Portugal has suffered chronic problems in forming and
sustaining coalitions. (Maxwell 1986, 6)

This situation has changed for the better in recent years, with the establishment of a majority government and a move toward a two-party
system.[8] At the same time, however, Portugal has been faced with another, more generally cultural problem which Jorge's novel implies and
which her later work addresses directly. The government's open-door
policy, established to offset the negative effects of nearly fifty years of
isolationism, is threatening to destroy what little remains of a national
identity. Hence, the situation of the nation as a whole in relation to
the rest of the world is beginning to take on an interesting parallel
with the "internal" relationship between the Algarve and Lisbon. For
that reason, Jorge's account of revolution coming to a remote village
can be understood as a way of imaginatively confronting the experience of the entire country, which is now feeling the full impact of
Western-style modernity.

Portugal has long felt the influence of countries such as England,
France, and Germany in its national life. But in recent years, the still
fledgling democracy has encountered a more serious threat to its stability, in the form of modern technology and the mass media. The
Brazilian telenovela, Hollywood movies, television series like "Dallas"
and "Dynasty," and rock videos are the most popular forms of enter-
tainment in Portugal today. One problem with the open-door policy is
that it threatens to turn Portugal into a cultural colony of the major
world powers, especially the United States. In effect, the nation is
faced with two equally unhappy alternatives: fascist isolationism or
absorption into a hegemonic, postcapitalist culture. To find a way out,
Portugal must discover a third alternative, which has not yet emerged.

During the last ten years, the Algarve has been the area in Portugal
where cultural change is most visible, chiefly because of tremendous
speculation by West European and British concerns. A good example
of the effect of foreign investment is Vilamoura, a name which sounds
ironically similar to Jorge's fictional village, but which is in fact a huge
five-star resort complex that includes hotels, condominiums, restau-
rants, shopping centers, a marina, and one of the most popular golf
courses in Western Europe. Unlike Albufeira or Faro, which existed
long before the tourist industry settled in, Vilamoura is the prototype
of a new kind of community. There is absolutely nothing Portuguese

about these places except their location; they are owned and inhabited by foreigners, and the principal language spoken, even by the Portuguese who work there, is English.

Jorge's concern for the survival of a Portuguese identity under these circumstances is suggested in *O Dia dos Prodígios*, especially in her attempt to mold a narrative technique that will respect the language and the culture of an Algarvian village, and in her use of an official peasant culture to comment ironically on official politics. But the problem of identity is even more clearly at the heart of her second novel, *O Cais das Merendas* (Picnic Quay) (1982), which throws certain aspects of the earlier book into sharp relief. *O Cais das Merendas* is also about the Algarve, but its primary concern is with the transformation of the rural population by the steadily growing multinational tourist industry. It tells about a group of villagers who come to the coast in search of employment and are hired to work in a hotel. Assimilated into this artificial environment, the former villagers can no longer fully communicate with the families they left behind; indeed, when relatives visit the hotel, they seem unusual and "quaint." As a result, the form of the novel subtly changes; the feeling of "magical realism" becomes much less apparent. Jorge's unusual techniques of rendering speech remain, but now the strangest events in the text have to do with the villagers' encounters with things like Hollywood movies.

Clearly, Jorge's work is meant to illustrate the difficult, paradoxical situation of a special part of her country, which is not only isolated from the national life, but is largely owned and populated by foreigners. Just as clearly, however, she is concerned with the nation itself. In commenting on the revolution and its aftermath, she has created one of the most unusual fictions of her generation, a powerful fusion of radically traditional and radically modern techniques which asks the reader—especially the Portuguese reader—to look for a third option, rethinking representation as well as history.

NOTES

1. Shortly after its publication, the book was reviewed enthusiastically in major newspapers, and it received the critical praise of established authors such as Vergílio Ferreira, Maria Teresa Horta, Urbano Tavares Rodrigues, and Baptista-Bastos. Jorge quickly became a prominent figure in the new

postrevolutionary literary group whose membership included, among others, the novelists Teolinda Gersão, António Lobo Antunes, José Saramago, Olga Gonçalves, and Hélia Correia. In 1983 and 1984, Jorge was awarded the Municipal Prize of Lisbon for her novels *O Cais das Merendas* (Picnic Quay) and *Notícia da Cidade Silvestre* (News from the Sylvan City). She recently finished a new book, *A Costa dos Murmúrios* (The Coast of Murmurs).

2. Jorge is in fact an admirer of Faulkner, but the comparison between them should not be pushed too far. Jorge is a left-wing writer, less romantic than Faulkner, less attracted to a biblical tradition, and separated from him by vast cultural differences.

3. There are certain affinities between Jorge's radical approach to speech and that of the Brazilian Ignácio de Loyola Brandão. See in particular his 1975 novel *Zero: Romance Pré-Histórico* (Zero: A Prehistoric Novel). João Guimarães Rosa, another Brazilian prose writer, experimented with the representation of speech in the 1950s, notably in a long prose piece entitled "Cara de Bronze" ("Bronze Face"). Consult his *No Urubùquaquá, no Pinhém* (1969).

4. See Mikhail Bakhtin, *Rabelais and His World* (1984, pp. 368–436). It should perhaps be emphasized that the war in Africa was an especially sensitive and often repressed topic in Portuguese society, not unlike the Vietnam War in America. Beginning in 1961, with a rebellion in Angola, the war quickly spread to other parts of Portuguese Africa and lasted until the takeover in April 1974. Like all colonial wars, it was waged in the name of Christianity and civilization, but the crude reality was that Portugal under Salazar was economically dependent on Africa as a supplier of inexpensive raw materials and as a market for its exports. From the beginning, the war was marked by unrest among the Portuguese officers in Africa, who resented that their counterparts at home, who occupied comfortable desk jobs, were being given more money and promotions. Their anger and frustration ultimately became the driving force behind the revolution.

5. For a recent discussion of the ideological status of conversation in novels, see Lennard J. Davis, *Resisting Novels* (1987, pp. 162–90).

6. The Portuguese writer Jorge de Sena had experimented with a double-column form in the mid-1960s in certain passages of his novella *O Físico Prodigioso* (The Wondrous Physician). Perhaps, significantly, Jorge's title is similar.

7. I have borrowed the term "presentational" from theater criticism, as a way of indicating a mode of address in which a dramatic speaker directly acknowledges the audience instead of pretending that the audience does not exist.

8. Although Portugal currently enjoys a measure of political stability, the period from 1974 to 1986 was in some ways disturbingly similar to the history

of the Portuguese Republic (1910–1926). The earlier attempt to establish a viable democracy was marked by continuous political upheaval which resulted in forty-five governments in a sixteen-year period. See Douglas Wheeler, *Republican Portugal: A Political History (1910–1926)* (1978).

IV

SEXUALITY AND REPRESSION IN HÉLIA CORREIA'S MONTEDEMO

Like Lídia Jorge, Hélia Correia writes about village life in twentieth-century Portugal, drawing on myths and indigenous folklore to describe people living on the fringes of the modern industrialized world. But unlike Jorge, whose early works are about the rural Algarve and its peasant population, Correia deals with a less specific region. The villages she describes seem typical of the nation as a whole, and many of her characters are either from a middle-class culture or are aspiring to it. Moreover, although both Jorge and Correia frequently invoke the supernatural, they use fantastic materials in totally different ways. Correia seems much less concerned with historical or political issues and less inclined to a radical estrangement of novelistic technique. She focuses instead on the emotional lives of provincial characters, and, as a result, her novels partake of a Gothic, psychological mode— sometimes involving Gothic themes in the context of realistic social satire and sometimes blending them with fantastic or folkloric motifs. By this means, she attempts to suggest what Sigmund Freud called the "return" of the repressed, especially in the sexual lives of women in small, puritanical communities.

What distinguishes Correia from other women writers of Gothic or fantastic literature in Portugal,[1] most of whom write about patriarchal repression, is precisely her interest in rural communities outside mainstream Portuguese society. Correia's fascination with a traditional, almost preindustrial world gives her work a special feel, as if the Gothic elements were being placed nearer to their origins in the Europe of the eighteenth and nineteenth centuries. At the same time, her fiction implies a modern, ironic distance from the events it describes; in one case, her recent novella *Montedemo* (Devil Mountain) (1983), her quasi-supernatural story takes on the quality of a satiric folktale.

In tentative ways, Correia can be related to the main tradition of Gothic literature, which includes the nineteenth-century Portuguese novelist Camilo Castelo Branco. Such fiction frequently involves provincial settings, partly because it seems to have arisen out of the romantic reaction against British and European industrialism; it is inevitably linked to a feudal aristocracy, if only in the form of decayed patriarchal houses; and in its early continental manifestations, especially in England, it expressed a latent nostalgia for the middle ages. In Gothic literature, ghosts and monsters mingled with castles, monks, and rooms filled with armor—an escapist, mysterious world far removed from the growing middle class. As the genre evolved, characters and settings became increasingly modern, and domestic settings of various kinds substituted for castles; nevertheless, the emphasis on the mysterious and the horrific remained, together with certain elements of the original mise-en-scène. (In England, for example, the popular novelist Daphne du Maurier was able to transpose the fictional materials of the Brontës into the contemporary estate which forms the background for *Rebecca*.) Large, multiroomed mansions with secret passages, locked attics, and creepy cellars have been typical of the genre, even though the modern characters are usually placed somewhere between a fading aristocracy and a new wealth. Significantly, too, the twentieth century has given Freudian motivation for the ghostly, fantastic events; the Gothic therefore evolved from a pure ghost story or tale of horror into a realistic type of psychological fiction, explicitly concerned with repression.

Even more pertinent to Correia's situation is the fact that so many women were attracted to the Gothic mode. Mary Shelley and the Brontë sisters were among the first writers to transform Gothic materials into "serious" literature, turning the conflicts and fears they experienced under patriarchy into *Frankenstein, Jane Eyre,* and *Wuthering Heights.* In fact, at the heart of what contemporary critics call the "Female Gothic"[2] is a constant tension stemming from society's contradictory notions regarding female sexuality, biology, and procreation; Gothic monsters and madwomen signify women's disquiet and unease regarding their own sexuality, to say nothing of their fears about their various and often conflicting roles as single women, married women, mothers, and daughters. The Gothic rooms and houses are emblematic of the repressed atmosphere in which the women characters live, with shadowy corridors, cellars, and attics indicating forbidden, unconscious regions. Thus while women writers retained the usual Gothic settings, they transformed them into something less escapist, more directly critical of bourgeois society.

Correia's early work takes this process a step further, introducing familiar themes of contemporary feminist fiction. She has kept vestiges of the original Gothic, but she tends to center on the middle-class "family drama," seldom depicting the household as nurturing and protective. Throughout her fiction, she describes the dark side of a domestic institution which, as the seat of male authoritarianism, represents the most immediately repressive force in women's lives[3]—often a road to psychosis or despair. Her first two novels seem more like purely realistic fiction; only in *Montedemo* does she make a partial return to a fantastic mode, as if to estrange her basic themes and reveal her sources. To show Correia's development, it may be useful to preface the analysis of *Montedemo* with a brief account of her earlier books.

Correia's first two novels, *O Separar das Águas* (The Parting of the Waters) (1981) and *O Número dos Vivos* (The Number of the Living) (1982), focus on middle-class women raised in the claustrophobic environment of the family and home. In both, Correia emphasizes the "madness" women face when they deny their sexuality and acquiesce to a way of life prescribed by the church and the narrow, provincial community. Correia also writes about women who are outcasts or who are in some way stigmatized by the community, rather like the "rebel" figures in early Gothic fiction. These characters—among them literal madwomen, witches, and gypsies—live mostly in the out-of-doors; they are sometimes regarded by the village as having supernatural powers, and their physical freedom provides an ironic contrast with the repressed lives of "normal" women confined to their homes.

The central female protagonists of these early novels are rarely seen outside the house. Maria Patrocínio and Maria Emília are rather like furnishings, although they are also expected to serve in the maintenance of the home. The extent to which the domestic situation becomes a prison, controlling their existence and demanding their allegiance, is suggested when Patrocínio, the protagonist of *O Separar das Águas,* jumps out of an upstairs bedroom window because she prefers to kill herself before having to admit that she has disgraced the family by becoming pregnant. Later, after she survives the fall, but loses the child, she marries her lover in order to redeem herself. However, marriage makes her life even more intolerable: not only is she forced to stay in the same house, she is now expected to accept the authority of her husband, who has moved into the family home and has replaced her father as master. Confined to the same structure, which for years dictated her course as daughter, Patrocínio must now take on a new, equally restrictive role as wife and mistress. Ultimately, opting for a life in the city where she is free, she leaves her husband and their recently born child. The villagers gossip about her driving around the city and smoking cigarettes, and they condemn her as corrupt and lost; in fact, her transgression against their moral and social codes is so great that officials in the village pronounce her dead. This punitive action effectively closes the door to any further discussion of Patrocínio's activities and, more importantly, to any speculation as to why she left her home. At the same time, the proclamation frees her husband to remarry and to bring another, less willful wife into the domestic prison. Thus, by "killing off" Patrocínio, the village fathers sanction and perpetuate repression; in effect, Patrocínio becomes a sort of ghost for the village, and the new wife becomes her Gothic double.

In *O Número dos Vivos,* Emília, the daughter of a peasant couple, aspires to middle-class status by accepting a position in a nearby village as companion to a well-to-do couple's only daughter, Romana. Emília's plan is to become so indispensable to the Saste's household that the family would fall apart without her. As the years go by, she masters all the domestic duties normally performed by the mistress of the house; finally, she runs the house and takes care of the entire family. Ironically, however, the daughter Romana rejects the home and family—everything that Emília has worked so hard to become part of and which to her signifies security. Breaking off her engagement to a socially prominent young man, Romana mysteriously disappears. The family learns later that she has joined a band of gypsies roaming the countryside; at this point, Emília assumes the role of daughter, since, in the eyes of the family, Romana is as good as dead. In fact, Emília finally marries Romana's fiancé and, like any good daughter, brings him to the house so she can continue caring for her "parents" while simultaneously taking on her new responsibilities as a married woman.

But what Emília believes to be the ideal role—the wife of a well-to-do man and the keeper of the keys—gradually becomes a living nightmare. Trapped in the family home while her husband is off in the city, she grows increasingly restless; she tries to vent her frustrations by composing fictional love letters to herself in order to make her less-than-ardent husband jealous. When he learns of her scheme, he abandons their bedroom and brings to a halt her already limited sexual activity. In retaliation, Emília seduces her father-in-law in the same bedroom once occupied by her and her husband, and she becomes pregnant. Upon learning of her condition, her father-in-law goes on an extended holiday; and following the birth, Emília's husband, who has taken up residence in the city, has her declared officially insane so he can divorce her without risking scandal. Emília's public disgrace forces her to remain within the confines of the home. As time passes, she loses interest in her domestic duties, and she finds her role as mother taken over by a young servant, the only person with whom the child speaks in her invented tongue. Finally, the strain of living indoors becomes too great for Emília, and she starts hallucinating. By the end of the novel, she is confined to her room, slowly sinking into madness.

The issues of maternity, female sexuality, and oppression raised in Correia's first two novels reappear in a slightly different form in her third and most interesting book to date, *Montedemo*, which is much more visibly connected to the Gothic and to fantastic fiction as a whole. Unlike her two earlier books, however, *Montedemo* is less concerned with individual or family dramas; it focuses instead upon an entire village's reaction to a forbidden sexuality. Moreover, Correia has moved the setting of her novella out of the traditional Gothic house and into the landscape, where "magical" events seem to occur in a purely natural world. *Montedemo* is like Lídia Jorge's *O Dia dos Prodígios* in that it is concerned with a relatively primitive, outdoor setting—a rural society which not only has close ties to the natural world, but also accepts without question utterly extraordinary occurrences. At the same time, *Montedemo* is different from Jorge's book;

here, the extraordinary or fairy tale events occur in an ambiguous bor-
derland between magical realism, satire, and psychological horror.
The powerfully lyric effect of her short text results from this ambiguity, as if the materials of Correia's early fiction had been transposed
into dream.

The fable-like quality of *Montedemo* is generated in part by the narrative strategy: a nondiegetic narrator retells a story which is already
part of the village folklore. The narrator's account begins with a description of a series of strange occurrences that happened there long
ago. One night the earth trembled; later, one afternoon, all the cats
fled the village; and not long afterward, for three days, the nearby sea
took the form of large, purple waves which stood absolutely still.
While most of the villagers were amazed and baffled by these events,
the more educated ones, like Tenório the pharmacist and Esteves the
clerk, tried to quell the mounting fear in the village by dismissing the
occurrences with rational explanations. For instance, they attributed
the purple waters to a special kind of seaweed which, under the right
conditions, gives off a reddish hue. (They further declared that the
same phenomenon was recorded in the Bible when Moses turned the
waters of the Nile to red.) The mysterious exodus of the cats they ex-
plained in terms of hormonal imbalances caused by seasonal changes.
In the case of the earth's tremor, some questioned if in fact it really
did occur.

The narrator recalls these magical events as if they were a natural
part of the village history, and uses them to prefigure an even more extraordinary occurrence which, we are told, happened on St. George's
Day some years ago. But before reviewing the events of that day, the
narrator fills us in on the history of a mountain, not far from the village, where the St. George festivities customarily took place. It seems
that the mountain was named "Montedemo" by the ancestors of
those now living in the village. For centuries it was the site of age-old
rituals celebrating life, death, and rebirth. Although the church condemned these pagan activities, the villagers continued to perform
them in secret. For example, young engaged couples would steal away
to the mountain late at night; pressing their bodies face down in its
fertile soil, they rubbed their bellies and mouths against Montedemo
as if it were a talisman to assure them of many healthy children.

Unable to dissuade the villagers from performing these fertility rituals, the local priest decided to baptize the mountain "São Jorge" (St.

George), hoping that its new name would somehow sanctify the pagan activity. He even tried to erect a chapel on the mountain in order to ensure, in a more concrete way, that whatever else took place there it would take place on blessed ground. But, according to legend, the mountain resisted the priest's conversionary tactics by sabotaging the construction. Avalanches and the mysterious disappearance of building materials brought the project to a hasty and unsuccessful close. After a time, even the name "São Jorge" fell out of use, and the mountain's original name, "Montedemo," was revived—much to the local clergy's dismay.

Clearly Montedemo represents a pre-Christian rite which the church tried to absorb into its own teachings, thereby repressing and disguising its original function. Described as a "bico enorme" (enormous peak), where seeds of all kinds frantically reproduce, Montedemo is the embodiment of sexual freedom and procreation which at once fascinates and frightens the local inhabitants. Not only is the mountain described in sexually explicit terms as "incha[ndo] e encolhe[ndo], como ofegante, como homem desvairado de desejo" (12) (swelling and contracting, panting like a man crazed by desire), it is also given a will of its own.

> Não há grande coragem que não comece logo a oscilar quando os beiços do monte sopram esse ar pesado que todos sabem negro embora pouca gente lhe tenha visto a cor, uma língua de morte que chamusca as laranjas e empalidece as fulvas flores dos cactos. E é esse um fraco aviso do coração do monte: para que fique seu o que seu é e ninguém tente abrir-lhe as veias e os segredos. (12)

> Even the most courageous souls tremble when the mountain's lips exude the heavy air that everyone knows to be black, although few have seen its color, a tongue of death that singes oranges and fades the tawny cactus flowers. And that pale warning from its heart is how the mountain keeps to itself what is its own: so that no one tries to open its veins and its secrets.

Montedemo is a force of supernatural power, and, like the Gothic architecture of nineteenth-century fiction, it is also a frightening erotic symbol. The similarities with the traditional Gothic, however, are only partial. As an architectural construct, the Gothic house connotes an attempt by civilization to restrain eroticism; whereas the mountain, which is outside society and actively opposed to any form of censure or control, represents sexuality and nature itself, which is unrepressed. The mountain also has a connotative power somewhat different from the more eerie eroticism in northern Gothic landscapes. Correia's imagery is made up of "black," "orange," and "tawny cactus," resulting in an almost Latin texture, a colorful use of the fantastic.

This view of the mountain as a scary, colorful, sexually uninhibited domain is further enhanced by the narrator's description of an incident that happened there years ago. What started out as a typical St. George's Day celebration on Montedemo ended in total disaster. At exactly three o'clock in the afternoon, in the midst of the festivities, a huge mass of thick, low-lying clouds rolled in over the mountain and blanketed the villagers' merriment. Suddenly, without any warning, their dancing and singing gave way to unprecedented acts of wild, sexual passion. When the clouds finally lifted, the villagers looked at one another, at first confused, then embarrassed, and then terrified by their total lack of restraint. Panicking, they fled Montedemo in droves. Casting frightened backward glances at the mountain, they raced toward the village, seeking the solace and security of their homes. For a long time no one spoke of what had happened on Montedemo that day—no one, that is, except Irene, the madwoman, who mocked the villagers' fearful silence by laughing in their faces while pointing in the direction of the mountain.

Irene, Correia's folksy version of the Gothic madwoman,[4] is not locked away in a distant room, like her sisters in some types of Gothic fiction. Even so, she has a similar function: she defies and ridicules "proper" social decorum. The book describes Irene in terms that emphasize her complete physical freedom: moving back and forth between the village and her hut near the sea, she continually roams about the countryside. One could argue that this is a simple reversal of the "madwoman in the attic" figure, suited to a tale which takes place mostly in the out-of-doors; thus, while Irene is not confined in the traditional sense, she is removed from the village and lives in relative isolation. But this argument does not respond to the question of her unlimited mobility in and outside of the community, nor does it explain why the villagers tolerate her antisocial behavior, which includes not only verbal abuse but also rock-throwing and other violent physical acts.

In order to understand Irene's function, we must first take into con-
sideration that Correia is not writing a typical Gothic work about
middle-class society. *Montedemo* is about a highly traditional, underdeveloped community which to some extent believes in the supernatural and practices pagan rites. Unlike the usual bourgeoisie, Correia's
villagers are still in awe of the natural world, whose presence is a dominant force in their lives. Within this less sophisticated culture, Irene is
not regarded as a social threat, even though her behavior is disturbing;
she is in fact a part of the village ritual—a somewhat mythic character
more like William Butler Yeats' "Crazy Jane." The villagers therefore
regard her as a force of nature, in the sense that her actions are beyond
their comprehension and control. This affinity between Irene and nature is suggested in Correia's descriptions, which portray the
madwoman "sniffing" out strangers who approach her cabin, "howl-
ing" at those who come too close, and communicating with animals.
In addition, Irene possesses certain magical powers which enable her
to decipher acts of nature and predict the future. Hence, the villagers
do not regard her madness as a social ill that needs to be contained.
On the contrary, they look upon Irene as a special creature endowed
with prophetic capabilities, who, although irritating and rebellious,
mediates between them and the natural world. In the case of the extraordinary occurrence on the mountain, however, the community
prefers to ignore Irene altogether; her mocking gestures are an uncomfortable reminder of their deviant sexual behavior.

While the villagers continue to avoid any mention of the St.
George's Day celebration, its impact on the community gradually
manifests itself in the form of two highly unusual events. The first involves Dona Ercília, a pious woman in her sixties, who is one of the
more socially prominent figures in the village. Prior to the incident on
Montedemo, Ercília spent her days knitting with other women in the
public square or gossiping with close friends over tea. After the infa-
mous celebration, however, Ercília broke contact with the outside
world and withdrew into the seclusion of her home where she fever-
ishly fingered her rosary beads. It seems that while on the mountain,
Ercília had "carried on" with a lottery ticket salesman named Tó—a
man who, under normal circumstances, she would not even acknowledge on the street. Cognizant of the gravity of her actions on the
mountain, which she keeps to herself, Ercília vows never to leave her
home until Tó drops dead—an event she prays will be imminent. The

villagers are mystified by her silent retreat; in a while, rumors circulate that she is suffering from a serious nervous disease and that she is constantly demanding to see the local parish priest.

Even more curious than Ercília's self-imposed seclusion is the change in her niece, Milena. For years Milena was rarely seen in the village, either keeping to herself in her room in her aunt's home or sitting inconspicuously in the shadows as her aunt and other women socialized in the out-of-doors. Suddenly, this sad, dowdy, thirty-year-old spinster, whom the village had basically written off, disappeared and was replaced by a "new" Milena—a vibrantly beautiful and smiling woman, who spent most of her time strolling about the village. Several months later the cause of this miraculous transformation became known. To the villagers' amazement, this woman, who rarely had spoken to a man, let alone had a serious relationship, was now pregnant. Shortly after this startling news broke, Milena left her aunt's home and settled in with Irene by the sea.

The village's reaction to this occurrence is somewhat strange because almost no one questioned how Milena became pregnant. Most of the villagers merely insist that she never showed the slightest interest in any of the local men. Although they are somewhat uneasy with the situation, they ultimately view her pregnancy as a miracle which, albeit baffling, is totally accepted. However, not everyone in the community is so easily appeased. Ercília, who is normally so preoccupied with herself that she is barely aware of her niece's presence, is dumbfounded by the rumors of Milena's condition, and she decides to investigate. Correia's description of this pious old woman turned inquisitor is wonderfully ironic. At the same time that Ercília recriminates herself for having committed sinful acts of the flesh, memories of which both shame and titillate her, she follows her niece around the house to find evidence of her guilt. Her investigatory tactics include smelling Milena's clothes to detect incriminating odors and whittling a hole in her bedroom door to peek at Milena while she undresses. One warm evening, Milena sheds all of her clothing before getting into bed. With her eye fastened to the peephole, Ercília finally sees the evidence of Milena's sexual transgression in the form of her "ventre redondo, tenso e resplandente" (round, taut, and resplendant stomach), which bore an uncanny resemblance to a "madrepérola" (mother-of-pearl) (28). Because Ercília cannot bear the thought of living under the same roof with Milena, whose pregnancy she regards

as a sin, she decides to ask her niece to leave. But when she finally
goes to Milena's room to make this request, she finds that her niece
and all her belongings have disappeared.

Milena's sudden, unperceived exit from her aunt's house to live
with the madwoman Irene is reminiscent of Romana's precipitous departure from the parental home in *O Número dos Vivos*. Not only do
both women reject the sexually repressed atmosphere of the house,
but also they opt for highly unconventional life styles in the untamed
out-of-doors. But it is not especially clear what prompts Romana, the
protagonist of the earlier novel, to take her drastic step. She is not
pregnant, and we know only that she is not interested in becoming a
wife or mother. She is merely withdrawn and imbued with a kind of
spiritualism that manifests itself as a glow emanating from her body;
her flight into the landscape is described as a highly mysterious disappearance, in keeping with a rather mystical transformation. In this regard, it is important to point out that Romana does not become a
religious recluse in the wilderness; rather, she joins up with a band of
gypsies and becomes one of their leaders. In other words, what was
perceived (or rationalized) by those around Romana as her religious
fervor and "glow" is in fact more like the manifestation of a frustrated
sexuality which gradually works its way to the surface.

Milena's situation is more complex than Romana's, since she becomes visibly pregnant while still living within the confines of the village. Clearly, Correia is satirizing a community which, initially
unaware of Milena's pregnancy, approves of her transformation from a
spinsterly type to a physically attractive woman, but then finds itself at
a loss as to how to view her in her new role as woman-about-to-be-
mother. As we all know, society has not been sympathetic with women
in Milena's situation, particularly not in the traditional Catholic society of rural Portugal. In this case, however, no one says anything
openly negative about Milena, even though "se sentiram pairar
morrinhas de pecado" (27) (they felt the symptoms of sin hovering in
the air). The villagers' silence on this issue is similar to that in the earlier novels, when Romana and Patrocínio are declared dead, even
though everyone knows they are alive. In all three cases, a puritanical
culture prefers simply to ignore or suppress issues regarding human
sexuality. In fact, the village in *Montedemo* manages successfully to
sidestep the issue of Milena's sexuality altogether by seeing her pregnancy as a miracle—a modern-day Immaculate Conception. Ercília,

whose strict religious upbringing makes her particularly sensitive to anything that smacks of evil, silently condemns Milena for violating church law; but she is treated as a comic stereotype, parodying the absurdly contradictory behavior of the sexually repressed. At the same time she openly professes moral "goodness," she is secretly drawn to and revels in the "perverse."

Milena's departure from the village coincides with the annual influx of summer tourists into the area; at this point, satire becomes infused with more truly fantastic events. Correia's description of the foreign invasion is mildly reminiscent of Lídia Jorge's *O Cais das Merendas*, which shows what happens when an isolated community is exposed to outside influences. Momentarily distracted by the tourists and their currency, the village at first fails to notice certain warning signals from nature, in the form of dead seagulls along the shore and strange voices moaning in the night. So preoccupied are the villagers with courting the tourists, that they gradually forget about Milena. Now the only ones aware of Milena's presence are some children, who wander out to where she lives, and a few couples, who seek the privacy of her isolated habitat to make love.

While Milena fades from the mind of the village as a whole, she attains a kind of cult status among those few children and adults who watch her in the water and on shore. As the following passage suggests, Milena seems at one with nature, a physically free being who personifies the erotic. Moreover, her refuge takes on a mystical quality similar to that of Montedemo: it inspires within those who visit an unprecedented feeling of intense physical passion:

> Viam-na sobre os altos das areias ou, mais longe, rompendo a flor da espuma. De ágeis pernas doiradas, orgulhosas, como colunas sustentando o mundo. Saltitava e sorria, detinha-se por vezes, de cabeça inclinada sobre o peito. E dimanava dela, do seu rasto, do seu voar de cabra um tal ardor que os pares de ocasião se consumiam em apetites nunca experimentados. O que fez com que as dunas, como antes certas pedras ou nós de algumas águas, passassem desde então por bênçãos de Afrodite. Dando aos corpos mais viço que gemas de ovo em mel ou cebolada. (32)

> They saw her over the tops of dunes or, farther off, breaking the crest of waves. Her golden agile legs, proud, like columns supporting the world. Skipping and smiling, she would pause at times, bowing her head

over her chest. And there emanated from her, from her trail, from her sprightly moves, an ardor so intense that the chance lovers were overwhelmed by desires never before felt. As a result, from that point on, the dunes, like certain rocks and some waters before, were considered blessings from Aphrodite. Giving bodies more vigor than either egg yokes in honey or onion stew.

After interpreting Irene's presence in his store and her agitation as a call for help with respect to Milena's condition, Tenório, the pharmacist, goes to the hut to check on Milena. He is struck not only by the smell inside, a blending of natural scents that has a curiously soothing effect on him, but also by Milena's "resinous" appearance within the glowing roundness of the cabin. Described in the book as a "seio erotizado" (eroticized breast), Milena's tranquil abode is the female counterpart of the awe-inspiring mountain whose "enormous peak" connotes aggressive male sexuality. Symbols of female and male eroticism, Milena and Montedemo are also linked by Correia's imagery. At one point in the book, Milena is described as wearing a green woolen cloak which makes her swollen belly appear like a *colina* or "hill." Notice, too, that this description carries within it the suggestion that she is pregnant by Montedemo.

There are further points of contact between Milena and the mountain. For example, just as the villagers seek out Montedemo under the cover of night, Tenório continues to visit Milena but only in the late evening and always clandestinely. As a result of his contact with her, Tenório undergoes a transformation. Once a sad, somewhat effeminate and repressed individual, Tenório is now happy and excited to the point that his sexuality is revived. But Tenório is not the only one to change as a result of his nightly excursions to Milena's home. Dulcinha Ferrão, a somewhat masculine-looking, older spinster, who decides to accompany Tenório on these nightly outings, becomes in the course of their adventure like a young girl, carefree and romantic. After a short while, Tenório and Dulcinha become lovers and decide to marry. This news rocks the village which, although it senses a change in the couple's behavior, finds their attraction to one another baffling and rather comic.[5]

But the villagers become distracted by an even more extraordinary occurrence which prefigures the birth of Milena's child. In spite of the autumn rains, fires break out in the village seven nights in a row. Curiously, the fires destroy only those things made of plastic, and they seem to have a special penchant for religious items, like saintly figurines, which they ferociously attack and melt down into distorted clumps. Equally perplexing is the fact that these unprovoked fires magically extinguish themselves before firemen can reach the scene. This week-long siege and the rumors that Tenório and Dulcinha are secretly roaming the countryside together strike a dissonant note in the community, which, finally free of the tourists, has reverted back to its more traditional and vigilant ways. In fact, at one point, a few villagers decide to follow Tenório and Dulcinha to the sea to find out what is going on. Just as they near the vicinity of the cabin, they are driven back by Irene, who, sensing their presence, breaks loose with a series of blood-curdling howls.

At last Milena delivers her child, but, to the shock of the community, the baby is black. What they had initially rationalized to be a kind of miracle has now, in their eyes, turned out to be a curse. They immediately recriminate themselves for not having seen in Milena's pregnancy the sign of evil at work. In an attempt to calm the majority's fear that some demonic spirit is in their midst, a few of the inhabitants suggest that perhaps Milena had simply become pregnant by one of the *retornados*.[6] But the frightened and excessively "respectable" members of the community flatly reject this possibility, claiming that since Milena never had the slightest interest in white men, it was highly unlikely that she would be sexually attracted to "aqueles negros bêbedos e pobres, carregados de filhos e incapazes de levar na conversa fosse que mulher fosse" (46) (those drunk and poor black men with children galore, who were incapable of conversing with whomever the woman might be).

By referring to *retornados,* Correia gives the exotic, almost fairy-tale quality of her narrative a sudden grounding in contemporary historical reality. In fact, her reference enables us to date the story in the years after the revolution, when thousands of Africans emigrated to Portugal. But more than just an historical reference, the villagers' comment reveals their racism and suspicion of outsiders—an attitude which seems to be consistent with puritanical superstition and a lingering racism in Portuguese society as a whole.

The villagers' inability to discuss sexual matters openly, or to acknowledge their own desires, has dire consequences. In this case, their repressed anxieties about Milena and her child resurface in the form of a skin disorder which plagues many in the community. As the threat of an all-encompassing evil becomes more and more real in their eyes, the villagers become increasingly hostile toward one another and more hysterical. Noninfected villagers avoid contact with those who suffer from the skin rash, convinced that the ailment is the manifestation of evil and is contagious. Finally, fearful that any kind of physical contact will result in disease, the entire community adopts a cautious attitude toward one another, especially the wives, who avoid their husbands, and the mothers, who keep their children at a distance. The description of these events becomes increasingly comic and absurd; the villagers' attempt to protect themselves from sin results in a scene where they buy up all the cleansers and disinfectants available and liberally douse everything in sight.

The villagers' fears turn into rage when they learn that Milena has been seen openly baring her breasts to feed her baby. Her nudity not only violates their sense of public decency, but also seems to them a deliberate challenge by the sinister forces at work in the community. Milena's disrobing outrages the population to such a degree that they decide to take measures to keep the evil she so clearly represents from spreading. At this point, Milena begins to resemble the Gothic "other" who, for the sake of society, must be contained or destroyed. Ironically, Tenório and Dulcinha are ecstatic about Milena's motherhood, and they view the baby as if he were their own. At one point the frightened villagers ask Tenório to explain how Milena came to give birth to such a child. This "new" Tenório is not concerned with allaying their fears; for him, the birth is a perfectly natural one and requires no explanation. Clearly, Tenório and Dulcinha no longer share the community's preoccupations with separating out "good" and "evil" or "right" and "wrong."[7] They merely accept what is, regardless of any moral criteria.

The climactic final scene in *Montedemo* bears a marked resemblance to certain dramatic scenes in Shelley's *Frankenstein*. The furious villagers set off to hunt down and destroy Evil, represented by Milena and her black child. But the villagers do not achieve their goal. Just as they close in, a deafening moan stops them in their tracks, and from the east, a blinding light pours forth from the mountain. The earth shakes, the sea turns red, and Irene's cabin goes up in flames; its three occupants disappear without a trace. A few months later, Irene reappears in the village, but she is now less agitated, more serene.

Tenório and Dulcinha are reported to visit Montedemo regularly, and from time to time a woman carrying a dark child has been seen on the mountain.

The narrator informs us early on that all these events happened long ago. In fact, however, we know that the novella is set in the very recent past, and the attempt to cast the story in the form of a folktale has ironic implications. The very form of the narrative is a sign of the villagers' attempt to forget its recent history, covering it over with the feel of myth. Indeed, according to the narrator, the apocalyptic events near the mountain have changed the whole life of the community, as if everything before were merely a dream. For example, the village has stopped going to the mountain altogether, and the St. George's Day festivities have been replaced by a cookout on a deserted beach to the north. Nowadays, we are told, little is said or known about the mountain. This does not mean, however, that the village is no longer aware of Montedemo or fearful of its wrath. On the contrary, from time to time, the inhabitants sense its awesomeness in the forms of rumblings and other signs which cause them to become nervous and afraid. Two things keep them from losing control in the face of the unknown: first, the sense of shame and guilt that has resulted from their own inexplicable behavior toward Milena and her child; and second, Tenório and Dulcinha's warnings that, if word got out that anything strange or unusual had occurred, the outside world just might bring in the dogs and tear gas. The story closes with Dulcinha's words "Amen-se" (Love one another), her counsel to the villagers and the moral of the tale.

The foregoing descriptive analysis treats *Montedemo* in largely thematic and formal terms, but to grasp fully the implications of the novella it is necessary to place it at least briefly in a social context. In this way we can see that Correia's mysterious, lyrical, tongue-in-cheek account of villagers caught up in a struggle with Evil is at bottom a critique of a more generalized puritanism and sexism in Portuguese society. The superstitions and repressions she describes are perhaps typical of provincial communities, but in an indirect way her fable concerns traditional mores of the country at large. After all, Portugal is not only a devoutly Catholic culture, but it was also ruled for decades by an officially puritanical and sexist dictatorship. Salazar had instituted both a political and a sexual censorship, banning all books that dealt explicitly or implicitly with erotic activity and creating an almost Victorian atmosphere of propriety. Even scientific works were kept out of the public's hands; the neurologist Egas Moniz's *A Vida Sexual* (The Sexual Life) was among those censored, despite the fact that, in 1949, he received the Nobel Prize (Robinson, 1979, 165). Furthermore, in Portugal there has always been a relationship between open discussions of sexuality and the larger struggle for democracy and women's rights. Thus the persecution of the Three Marias, which began shortly after the publication of *Novas Cartas Portuguesas*, had centered largely on the explicitly sexual content of their work. The charge against the three women was not "feminism" (although this was clearly the real danger to the regime), but "obscenity." Their arrest and public trial were, in the early stages, concerned precisely with the question of what writers could say about an officially secret erotic life.

While Correia's novella was of course written after the revolution, it does not deal with sex in especially graphic terms. Nevertheless, like all her works, it concerns women's sexual desire—particularly the threat posed by women's sexuality to a repressed, patriarchal community. This theme remains an important one because, despite the fact that the Portuguese dictatorship ended in 1974, old habits die slowly. Even today women walking alone down a Lisbon street in full daylight can hear the kiss-kissing sounds from male bystanders. *Montedemo* traces such a phenomenon to its roots, in the values of a society where middle-class women were once expected to stay almost exclusively in the home. These old values are less visible in cosmopolitan cities, especially today, but they survive in isolated communities throughout the countryside. Correia is therefore able to write a fiction that seems in some ways to partake of a truly nineteenth-century Gothicism.

Unlike Lídia Jorge, Correia does not view provincial life in complex, problematic terms. Her attitude toward her fictional village is more purely satiric, and the village itself is a generalized world rather than a specific region. The reader feels a relatively comfortable, ironic distance from the strange events in the tale and is able to interpret them fairly easily. At the same time, however, the historical and cultural situation of Portugal gives Correia an opportunity to invest her satire on sexual repression with a highly romantic, magical aura. In a nation where progressive modernity coexists with a very old provincial society, her feminist thematic can take on the quality of folktale or legend. The result is an unusual and quite compelling fiction, in which a contemporary social critique merges with a lyric and mysterious style.

NOTES

1. Within the last ten years, a number of Portuguese women authors have either partially or fully dedicated themselves to the writing of fantasy literature. Among these are Maria Isabel Barreno, Maria Ondina Braga, Maria Teresa Horta, Maria Velho da Costa, Olga Gonçalves, Luísa Costa Gomes, Clara Pinto Correia, and Maria Regina Louro. For a representative sampling of their works in this genre, see *Fantástico no Feminino* (Fantastic in the Feminine) (Lisbon: Editora Rolim, 1985).

2. The idea of a "Female Gothic" originated with Ellen Moers whose book *Literary Women* (1976) contains a chapter on the subject. For a more recent discussion of this genre, consult *The Female Gothic*, edited by Juliann E. Fleenor (1983).

3. See Barbara Hill Regency, *Madness and Sexual Politics in the Feminist Novel* (1978), p. 9, for her comments on the psychologist R. D. Laing's theory about women and the authoritarian family unit.

4. The madwoman figures prominently in a number of Gothic tales; *Jane Eyre*'s Bertha Mason is perhaps the best-known example. For generations, critics saw her as the embodiment of evil—a willful, sensual woman who scorned the passive, nurturing roles that society expected her to assume. She is punished for her actions by being locked away in a tower room—her husband Rochester's only recourse to protect himself and others from the consequences of her wicked ways. More recently, feminist critics have rejected this view of Bertha as evil—seeing in her, the madwoman, the "other" side of female behavior which society teaches women to suppress. As more than one critic has noted, Bertha is the rebellious counterpart of the angelic Jane—the "other" which, to be successful in the world, Jane must hold in check.

5. Not only are Tenório and Dulcinha a variation on the nursery-tale Jack Spratt and his wife, but they are also androgenous figures: Dulcinha is like a "sargentão" (a big sergeant) and Tenório is not only slim but also highly affected. This unlikely pair is reminiscent of Carson McCullers' bizarre androgenous couple—a muscle-bound man-woman who falls in love with a diminutive hunchback—in her Gothic novel, *The Ballad of the Sad Café* (1951).

6. The term *retornados* (returnees) generally refers to refugees from the former Portuguese colonies in Africa. In Correia's story, however, the villagers are applying the term to the blacks who emigrated after independence.

7. In the introduction to *The Female Gothic*, the authors contend that the Gothic is created by "the social division of women into either pure and chaste or impure and corrupt" (p. 15).

V

THE LANGUAGE OF SILENCE IN TEOLINDA GERSÃO'S O SILÊNCIO

I want to write a novel about Silence . . . the things people don't say. But the difficulty is immense.

Virginia Woolf, *The Voyage Out*

Teolinda Gersão's brief novel *O Silêncio*, published in 1981, has been compared to Clarice Lispector's *Perto do Coração Selvagem* (Close to the Savage Heart), which appeared thirty-seven years earlier in Brazil. The comparison is apt, since the two books have similar characters and both are preoccupied with the theme of silence. But the classic statement on the paradox of meaningful silence was written by Virginia Woolf, in the lines quoted above from *The Voyage Out*, her first novel, which was composed in the years immediately before the First World War. Although Woolf places these lines in the mouth of a young novelist named Terence Hewet, many critics have observed that they seem prophetic of her own later fiction and of literary modernism as a whole. Indeed, where women's literature is concerned, it is probably correct to say that silence of one kind or another has been a central topic throughout the twentieth century, requiring writers to adopt a paradoxical language.

I do not know whether Teolinda Gersão ever read Woolf's novel, but it is clear that these two women, widely separated in time and cultural background, have certain interests in common. In fact, the scene in *The Voyage Out* where Hewet speaks his famous lines has a number of striking affinities with a scene near the beginning of *O Silêncio*, and the two passages deserve an extended comparison.

The episode in Woolf's novel centers on a conversation between Hewet and a young middle-class woman named Rachel, whom Hewet wants to know better. In an attempt to draw her out, Hewet asks Rachel to describe her life in England (the novel takes place in South America). In the course of talking about her daily activities, which are largely domestic, Rachel stops twice—both times to apologize to Hewet for the trivial nature of her conversation. Hewet reassures her that he is deeply interested in what she has to say. When Rachel asks him why, he replies, "Partly because you're a woman," and then elaborates on his remark:

> "I've often walked along the streets where people live all in a row, and one house is exactly like another house, and wondered what on earth the women were doing inside. . . . Just consider: it's the beginning of the twentieth century, and until a few years ago no woman had ever come out by herself and said things at all. There it was going on in the background, for all those thousands of years, this curious, silent unrepresented life. Of course we're always writing about women—abusing them or jeering at them, or worshipping them; but it's never come from women themselves. I believe we still don't know what they feel, or what they do precisely. . . . It's the man's view that's represented, you see. Think of a railway train: fifteen carriages for men to smoke. Doesn't it make your blood boil? If I were a woman I'd blow some one's brains out." (Woolf 1965, 258)

Interestingly, *O Silêncio* begins with a long narrative passage in which the character, Lídia, imagines a roughly equivalent scene. In Lídia's imagination, a man and woman are talking, and the woman tries to communicate on a level deeper than "the language of love." But she senses, even before she begins to speak, that the man will resist this different kind of dialogue. She therefore decides to begin the conversation on a very general, almost superficial level, using "palavras que ofereciam espaços livres, onde a forma dela própria podia sempre perder-se de vista facilmente, no meio de uma infinidade de outras coisas" (12) (words that offered wide-open spaces, where

her own form could always easily be lost sight of, in the midst of an in-
finity of other things). She then plans to direct the conversation gradually to a "limited space," or to her own world, and it is at this point
that the dialogue will assume the intensity she seeks.

Lídia's imagined scenario, in which a woman looks for an unconventional language outside ordinary dialogue, is replayed over and
over in O Silêncio, especially when Lídia tries to find ways to discuss
her private feelings with her lover Afonso, who either refuses to listen
or listens skeptically. But the opening scene also has specific features
in common with the passage in Woolf's book. For instance, both texts
involve a man and woman at the edge of the sea. (In The Voyage Out,
Hewet and Rachel are on a cliff overlooking the ocean, and in O
Silêncio Lídia's imagined couple are on the beach.) In both passages, a
character of one sex is attempting to know the other sex in a more profound way, and the language these characters use is often strikingly
similar. Asked to talk about her life, Rachel speaks mainly of the home
and of the daily round of breakfast, lunch, and tea; when she pauses,
somewhat embarrassed at the "trivialities" she describes, Hewet urges
her to continue, saying: "Go on, please, go on . . . Let's imagine it's a
Wednesday. You're all at luncheon. You sit there, and Aunt Lucy
there, and Aunt Clara here . . ." (256). In O Silêncio, the woman's
speech also involves a description of a domestic ritual. At one point,
the man asks the woman to elaborate, saying: "Conte o que se passou
numa quarta-feira qualquer" (17) (Tell what happened on any given
Wednesday). Like Rachel, the woman goes on to describe a typical
Wednesday, evoking a scene in which three individuals sit around in
the late afternoon drinking coffee. Finally, both scenes come to a
close with the mention of time. In The Voyage Out, Rachel exclaims:
"It must be late!" (265); in O Silêncio, the imaginary scene suddenly
ends when a man says to Lídia: "É tarde" (20) (It's late). There is also
an equivalent sense of disappointment that follows upon the attempt
to communicate: Hewet feels dissatisfied that he and Rachel spent
too much time talking about unimportant things; Lídia's discontent
is expressed indirectly as she watches grains of sand run through her
fingers, helpless in the face of their flow toward nothingness.

Although there are several parallels between the two passages, it
should be pointed out that there are also important differences in the
ways in which Woolf and Gersão approach their subjects. One of the
most significant differences has to do with form—not only the form

of their respective texts, but also the form of the dialogue spoken by their characters. In *The Voyage Out*, the discussion between Hewet and Rachel is depicted in terms of the usual conventions of realist fiction—this despite the fact that the two characters are talking about the impossibility of communicating through established conventions. Even when the speech between the two characters becomes somewhat groping and difficult, it is always conducted in the polite, rational fashion of the British upper class. In contrast, Gersão allows us to read all statements as the thought of a character named Lídia rather than as literal speech, thus making the language on the page doubly silent. On the one hand, the dramatized characters cannot say what they mean; on the other hand, their words are only remembered or imagined, never directly voiced. In fact the situation in the novel is still more complex because it is often difficult to know whose thoughts are being represented: exactly which words belong to Lídia, and which to the woman she imagines? Gersão also gives the woman in Lídia's imagined scene a strange sort of language; when this character attempts to describe "any given Wednesday," she begins with mundane details which lead into a kind of fairy tale, in which two of the characters fly off on broomsticks. Throughout, her language has a free-associative, fantastic quality and is composed of disparate things: a stream of water running down a wall, a cat jumping over a gate, a house with a garden. At one point, she talks about a kind of garden solar system and a house that, like a sunflower, turns according to the position of the sun. Suddenly she refers to some people in a house and to a discussion between two men, Herberto and Alfredo, about a woman, Lavínia, who flees the house with Herberto only to return some time later to Alfredo, who is crying in a train station.

Unlike the Woolf passage, there is no apparent logic or order in this scene. It begins with a character imagining a woman and man talking; the woman in turn imagines another scene in which two people speak. The entire narrative creates the effect of a *mise-en-abyme*, a form which is alluded to in the woman's description of some gardens which "fundem-se uns nos outros e não se sabe bem onde começam e acabam" (14) (merge one into the other not knowing quite where they begin or end). It should also be noted that early on in the imaginary conversation, the man tries to impose a logic on what the woman is saying by drawing a diagram in the sand of a house with a garden and a cat sitting on a wall—a picture that proves to be inaccurate and finally incapable of representing all that the woman has to say. Ulti-mately, her language seems to have no boundaries and it defies coher-ence or order.

Woolf's technique in her early fiction is paradoxical; it can refer to meaning only in terms of silence or the space between words, but it re-tains the orderly, rational forms of traditional discourse. Woolf's later experiments, like Gersão's book, might be described as an alternative strategy—an attempt to make silence or repressed meaning audible by means of an unorthodox technique. Paradoxically, her last novel, *Be-tween the Acts*, speaks of the need to render life in the form of "scraps, orts, and fragments," and the technique we find in Gersão's O Silêncio could be described in exactly those terms. Indeed Gersão's small book is so utterly fragmented, so strange in form, that it poses considerable problems for the reader. Before discussing the events it depicts, it may be useful to analyze its perplexing surface.

O Silêncio is divided into three sections, each of which is preceded by blank pages on which the numbers 1, 2, and 3 appear, respectively. But this apparent marking off of a beginning, middle, and end seems at most a playful or ironic device, since the multiple prose fragments within each section do not follow any particular chronology or narra-tive development. Altogether there are sixty-two short blocks of lan-guage in the novel (twenty-three in part 1, sixteen in part 2, and twenty-three in part 3), which range from several pages in length to a single line; each is separated by a blank space. At one level, the book gives us a sense of linearity, represented by the chronologically num-bered sections and by the blank gaps which serve as silent pauses or interludes between the fragments; at another level, it seems to col-lapse time and space, providing us with little more than a series of dis-jointed passages in which characters and events past and present commingle and coalesce.

Although the setting is a contemporary one, no dates are given, and no references or allusions are made to historical events that might place the action of the novel within a more specific frame of time. Sea-sons are mentioned, but they do not follow any chronological order. Words such as *dia, tempo, momento,* and *agora* abound, but they ap-pear in such a general context and in such a plotless fashion that they almost lose their meanings. In similar fashion, no single voice or nar-rative perspective unifies the text. We shift back and forth among at least four characters, but these characters, who are themselves fragmented, often adopt different voices when they speak: sometimes they talk about their experiences in the first person, sometimes in the second person, and sometimes in the third. Frequently, the different points of view and different modes of address appear within a single fragment, which leads to a great deal of confusion. For example, one passage begins and ends with a character speaking in the first person and addressing another character as "you"; if we read the passage carefully, however, we discover that the narrating "I" is not the same character throughout, nor is the "you" who is being addressed. A related problem surfaces when fragments are narrated in the third person: a passage will often begin with what seems to be the conventional extradiegetic narrator of nineteenth-century fiction, but then the voice is discovered to be one of the characters, who is speaking about himself or herself. Then, within the same section, a character's "monologue" can shift into the first person. In other words, a character can function as both the object and subject of his or her own narration, so that in any given passage the "he" or "she" and the "I" of a particular discourse might refer to the same individual. There are seldom any cues alerting the reader to these shifts in perspective and voice—they might happen anywhere, sometimes forcing the reader to reorient himself or herself several times within a single fragment.

The shifting point of view and the different modes of address become even more confusing given the fact that many times a fragment will begin with no indication of who is speaking or whose thoughts are being recorded. In some instances, the pronouns *ele* (he) and *ela* (she) are the only clues to the source of narration—and these are not much help since the book concerns several individuals. Even the appearance of a character's name does not necessarily orient us since the names of the two principal women characters (Lídia and Lavínia) and of the two principal male characters (Alfonso and Alfredo) are so similar that they tend to blur together in the reader's mind like Tweedledum and Tweedledee. (One early review of the novel mistakenly identified the main character as "Lívia"—an interesting amalgamation of the two women's names.)

Many of the fragments are narrated from a first-person perspective, but it is not clear if what is being said is spoken aloud by the character as a kind of soliloquy, or is only imagined or remembered in the character's interior monologue. This ambiguity extends to what seems like dialogue. Sometimes "conversations" suddenly appear in the middle of a sentence, as in the example below:

> Subiu do mar, contornou o cais, voltou descalça por sobre as pedras, sentou-se ao lado, ofegante ainda, escorrendo água, um cardume negro passou, rápido, muito perto da superfície, mil peixes, disse ela seguindo-os com os olhos, cem peixes, disse ele cem peixes apenas, passou uma das mãos nos seus cabelos molhados, fez deslizar os dedos ao longo do seu rosto . . . (48)

> She came out of the sea, rounded the pier, returned barefoot over the rocks, sat down at the side, still panting, water dripping, a black school of fish passed by, rapidly, very close to the surface, a thousand fish, she said, following them with her eyes, one hundred fish, he said, only one hundred, he drew one of his hands through her wet hair, and ran his fingers down alongside her face . . .

Gersão's long, run-on sentence style enables her not only to fuse different perspectives and voices, but also to embed quotation within narration, giving the impression that a conversation has momentarily surfaced in the midst of a stream of consciousness. In other places she seems to blend two voices together, so that what looks at first like "thought" ultimately becomes a sort of "speech":

> Onde poderá estar o meu botão de punho, se já se procurou em todos os armários, todas as caixas, todas as gavetas, debaixo de todas as camas, não sairei jamais sem o botão de punho, mas você não tem outro, mesmo diferente, mas não se podem usar botões diferentes, já viu alguém com um braço azul e outro verde, você faz de propósito, para criar o caos à minha volta, onde é que você pôs os esticadores da camisa . . . (82–83)

> Where can my cufflink be, if one's already looked in all the closets, all the boxes, all the drawers, under all the beds, I'll never leave without my cufflink, but don't you have another one, even if it's different, but different cufflinks can't be worn, have you ever seen someone using one that's blue and the other green, you're doing this on purpose, to create chaos around me, where did you put the collar tabs for my shirt . . .

Occasionally, Gersão uses paragraphing to separate one character's words from another, but her unusual form of punctuation makes even this traditional way of representing dialogue seem strange:

> O absurdo de tudo isso, disse Afonso, a paixão da paixão, a procura da procura, o desejo em último caso sem objecto, porque o seu objecto é o desejo e nada do que você conta, ou diz, ou sonha, existe,
> o medo do amor, disse ela, o medo que você tem de ir até ao limite de si próprio, de destruir tudo o que fica para trás e criar em seu lugar outra coisa, (99)

> The absurdity of all that, Alfonso said, the passion for passion's sake, the search for the search alone, the desire ultimately without any object, because neither its object, nor the desire, nothing that you tell, say, or dream exists,
> the fear of love, she said, the fear that you have of going to the limits of your own self, of destroying all that which is left behind and creating in its place something else,

The comma ending each paragraph and the lack of a capital letter in the second paragraph make the speeches merge, or perhaps they suggest that the characters' words to one another continue beyond what is recorded on the page. Note, too, that while the speakers address their remarks to one another, the overall effect seems less like a conversation and more like two monologues, one overlapping the other, in which recriminations are registered in a poetic, litany-like fashion.

A more traditional looking dialogue appears in a long fragment near the beginning of the book. The fragment starts with what seems to be an authorial voice, but the first paragraph ends with the words "eu quero" (I want), transforming everything that has gone before into the subjective narration of a character. At the very moment the first-person voice is introduced, the fragment suddenly becomes a dialogue—the only place in the book where indenting and dashes appear, indicating direct quotation:

> O silêncio do mar, as dunas frias, a praia deserta, o vento nas noites longas. As palavras arrumadas num pequeno espaço, um quadrado para cada letra, uma rede diminuta prendendo a desordem aparente,

apenas aparente. A revista de novo fechada, dobrada no cesto de vime,
o relógio batendo, e não é nada disto que eu quero,
   —recusar tudo e recomeçar de outra forma,
   —mas não há outra forma possível,
   —corpos que brevemente se entendem e de novo partem, soltos,
separados,
   —porque você recusa o real, você recusa
   —porque sempre sonhei viver de outro modo,
   —mas só existe o real e é preciso resignar-se,
   —mas quem vai definir o que é real,
   —o real é o contrário do sonho,
   —e se for o sonho que é real,
   —está de novo mentindo,
   —a vida não se repete apenas, é possível uma súbita alteração qualitativa,
   —a vida é uma coisa sem brecha, mas não há nunca rotura nem milagre,
   —não sonhamos talvez o suficiente,
   —é preciso parar de imaginar.
   —Vou-me embora, disse-lhe, depois de uma pequena pausa, mas ele
riu e recostou-se para trás, apoiando melhor a cabeça sobre os braços
cruzados nas costas da cadeira. (36—37)

The silence of the sea, the cold dunes, the deserted beach, the wind
in the long nights. The words neatly arranged in a small space, a square
for each letter, a tiny network holding together the apparent disorder,
merely apparent. The magazine once again closed, folded in the wicker
basket, the clock striking the hour, and it isn't any of this that I want,
   "to reject everything and begin again in another form,"
   "but there isn't any other form possible,"
   "bodies that briefly come together and then part once again, separated and free,"
   "because you refuse the real, you refuse,"
   "because I always dreamed of living another way,"
   "but only the real exists and it's necessary to resign oneself,"
   "but who is going to define what is real,"
   "the real is the opposite of the dream,"
   "and if it were the dream that is real,"
   "you're lying again,"
   "life doesn't merely repeat itself, a sudden qualitative change is possible,"
   "life is a thing without gaps, there is never rupture nor miracle,"
   "perhaps we don't dream enough,"
   "it's necessary to stop imagining."
   "I'm going away," she said to him, after a brief pause, but he laughed

and leaned back, supporting his head on his arms which were crossed
on the back of the chair.

Despite the conventional paragraphing and dashes, this is a curious
form of dialogue. The voices seem to be coming out of nowhere in particular, and there is no mention of who is speaking to whom. The
lower case letters at the beginning of each line and the commas at the
end suggest that what we are hearing is part of an exchange which
closes with the period at the end of "é preciso parar de imaginar," but,
because of the unusual manner of speech and punctuation, it is difficult to say exactly what is being represented. Is this an actual conversation, or is it a conversation recalled or imagined in the character's
mind? The line, "—Vou-me embora, disse-lhe . . .", looks realistic because it begins with a capital letter and it is followed by a brief, dramatic description of another character's physical response to the
words. But the relationship between this line and the previous exchange is not clear; one possibility is that the lines "quoted" after the
initial paragraph are only imagined by the woman who speaks the
phrase "I'm going away." The final comment is therefore articulated
out loud, and is motivated by another, silent conversation.

The interpenetration of private and public speech is in fact a central issue in the novel. Repeatedly, Gersão depicts scenes in which a
woman cannot make herself heard by a man, so that she is forced into
a kind of free-association monologue or into silence. For example, in
section one, Lídia and Afonso speak to one another while a record
plays in the background. Their exchange is prefaced by a monologue
in which Lídia talks (or thinks) about Afonso, about herself, and
about their relationship. When the conversation begins, the characters' words are merely set off in separate paragraphs, with no dashes to
indicate quotation. Lídia talks about a possible future existence where
speech will no longer exist, and she seems to ramble on at length. By
contrast, in the space of three pages, Afonso makes only four brief
comments. Lídia's words are presented in the form of a surreal,
run-on speech about an impending crisis of silence, and at one point
she talks about a world of the future in which people who feel the need
to talk will wear little green ears on their lapels. Afonso responds sar-
donically, wondering aloud what the manufacturer of the first green
ears will earn ("imagine o que irá ganhar or primeiro fabricante de
orelhas verdes" [40]); then, in response to another long speech by

Lídia, in which she imagines a world taken over by computers, he says, "é você que ironiza ... e depois acusa-me de não falar a sério" (41) (it's you who are being ironic ... and then you accuse me of not speaking seriously). As Lídia continues to talk about a strange world of the future, Afonso puts a record back in its album cover ("com cuidado, ele tornou a pôr o primeiro disco no lugar, depois de o meter no invólucro de plástico e na capa brilhante de papel" [41]) and then, waving his pipe to the music as if it were an imaginary baton, tells Lídia to pay attention to the mandolin solo ("repare no solo de mandolinas" [41]). The fragment ends with Afonso laughing out loud—"está a ver como está a mentir, desde o início" (do you see how you are lying, from the very beginning)—and his laughter is described as ("so[ando] como um canto de alívio e vitória sobre todas as palavras ditas" (42) (sounding like a song of relief and victory over all the words said).

These curious renditions of failed or blocked communication between a woman and a man are summarized in the final section of the book, where we encounter a fragment in which a question is asked and a response is given. There is barely any indication of the speakers, and there is no way of knowing whether what is being said is being spoken out loud. The line as it first appears is as follows:

Em que está a pensar? perguntou-lhe. Em nada, disse. (99)

What are you thinking about? he asked her. Nothing, she said.

Three pages later, the fragment reappears in the following form:

em que está a pensar?, perguntou-lhe. Em nada, disse. (102).

If we look back at the middle of the book, we find the same line is embedded in the middle of a longer fragment in which Lídia is talking about herself in the third person:

... Por vezes ele surpreendia-a distraída, pensando em coisas, e atirava bruscamente a pergunta, como se lhe pegasse pelos ombros, de repente: em que está a pensar? Em nada, dizia sempre. (61)

... At times he surprised her in her distraction, thinking about things, and brusquely threw out the question, as if he were all of a sudden shaking her by the shoulders: what are you thinking about? Nothing, she always said.

"Nothing" in this case is simply another word for a woman's voiceless language. Throughout, *O Silêncio* has tried to represent a paradoxical phenomenon, which turns silence into a kind of speech. If we now consider the story that emerges from the novel's fragmentary prose, we can better understand the motive for Gersão's unusual technique.

O Silêncio focuses on two middle-class couples—Lídia and Afonso and Lavínia and Alfredo—whose lives are intertwined. The exact nature of the relationship between these couples, however, is withheld until the end of the novel, where Lavínia is indirectly revealed to be Lídia's mother.

The novel devotes most of its attention to Lídia and Afonso, although only bits and pieces of their history are revealed. We know that Lídia was at one time reluctant to enter into a relationship with Afonso, who was a married man. Afonso, however, was extremely eager to become her lover; frustrated with his marriage and his job as a doctor, he saw Lídia as his last chance for happiness. Therefore he abandoned his wife, Alcina, and their home, took up residence in an apartment across a bridge from where Lídia lived, and waited for her to come to him. In reflecting upon this moment in their lives, Afonso feels extremely satisfied with himself for having conquered Lídia—a victory that saved him from what had become a lifeless existence.

While Afonso considers himself the victor, theirs is a tense, embattled relationship. What first attracted Afonso to Lídia—her spontaneity, unpredictability, and disorder—now seems unattractive and even destructive, in conflict with her new role as woman of the house. Lídia resists domestication, and she is determined to rid Afonso of his obsession with orderliness and complacency; but he repeatedly tries to make her over in the image of her predecessor, Alcina, who spent her life indoors, making certain everything was in its proper place.

The novel is filled with vivid contrasts between these two; its pattern of imagery tends to associate Lídia with nature and Afonso with culture. Lídia has an affinity with the out-of-doors, especially with large, open spaces free of any restraints or limitations. The sea is her preferred abode, and she seems to bring the random disorder of the seaside into the household:

Escalar as dunas, transpirar subindo, agarrada à vegetação rasteira, parar arquejante a meio, o mar de repente encoberto pelo chapéu largo de palha . . . sentar-se na primeira pedra e ver o mar, atirar o chapéu para o lado e levantar a cabeça contra o vento, gritar ou cantar ou ficar calada, olhando o mar . . . voltar finalmente para casa sobraçando um cesto de flores e camarinhas bravas, empurrar a porta e reencontrar Afonso— . . . e ela poisa ao acaso o cesto que acabara sempre por tombar e aproxima-se descalça, pisando a areia que se solta do seu corpo e as flores que se espalharam pelo chão. E a desordem é subitamente uma forma de amor, a sua forma de amor. Interromper Afonso como o mar entrando.(22)

To scale the dunes, to perspire climbing, holding on to the low-lying vegetation, stopping midway panting, the sea suddenly concealed by the large straw hat . . . to sit down on the first rock and watch the sea, throwing the hat to the side and raising her head against the wind, to scream or sing or be quiet, looking at the sea . . . finally to return home carrying a basket of flowers and berries under her arm, to push open the door and meet Afonso again— . . . and she carelessly puts down the basket that always ends up falling over, and she approaches barefoot, stepping on the sand shaken loose from her body and on the flowers scattered about the ground. And the disorder is suddenly a form of love, her form of love. To interrupt Afonso like the sea entering.

Lídia is not at all concerned with having a neatly arranged house, and she always keeps the windows and drapes open so that she can feel the chaos of the out-of-doors. Afonso, on the other hand, is not at all happy unless there is absolute domestic order; he makes a point of closing the windows and drapes, and his favorite room is his perfectly organized study, where his records and books are arranged in alphabetical order.

Lídia is a completely spontaneous character whose actions are as sudden and unpredictable as the natural forces around her. At one moment, she is scaling a sand dune; at the next, she is perched quietly on a rock gazing out to the sea. At any given time, she might burst into song, scream, or be totally still. Meanwhile, Afonso executes even the most casual actions in methodical fashion:

Levantou-se, depois, procurou um disco na estante, retirou-o da capa de papel brilhante e do invólucro transparente de plástico, colocou-o no prato do gira-discos, encontrou sem olhar, apenas estendendo

ligeiramente uma das mãos até a parte inferior da estante, um pedaço
de camurça fina (o instinto da ordem, a segurança de cada coisa,
sempre facilmente manejável, no lugar certo), pôs o disco a girar e
limpou-o ao de leve, imobilizando sobre ele a mão que segurava a
camurça, finalmente fez descer a agulha, com um mínimo de pressão,
até um ponto aparentemente invisível na primeira estria negra e circular, que era contudo o ponto exacto da primeira nota de música.
(37–38)

He got up, then looked for a record on the shelf, took it out of the
brightly colored album cover and removed it from the plastic cover inside, placed it on the turntable, and without looking but by merely ex-
tending lightly one of his hands back into the shelf, finding a piece of
fine chamois cloth (the sense of order, the security of each thing, always easily manageable, in its proper place), he set the record turning,
gently cleaning it, his hand holding the chamois completely still over
the record, finally he lowered the needle, with a minimum of pressure,
to a point apparently invisible on the first black circular band, that was
also the exact point of the first note of music.

In one respect, the novel is about the impossibility of these two individuals finding happiness together. As the reader learns early on in
the book, theirs are "dois mundos sem pontos de contacto" (34) (two
worlds without points of contact), a fact which both characters have
known since the beginning of their relationship. But this realization
does not prevent them from trying to draw one another into their respective worlds, and their struggle to achieve the impossible constitutes one of the central themes in the novel.

The relationship between Lídia and Afonso is in certain ways paralleled with that of the second couple, Lavínia and Alfredo. Alfredo, a
Portuguese teacher, went to Paris, where he met a Russian emigré; he
married her and brought her and her small daughter back with him to
his home. Upon coming to Portugal his wife adopted the name
"Lavínia" because her given name proved too difficult for people to
pronounce. She experiences considerable difficulty in learning the
language, a problem exacerbated by the fact that Alfredo is her in-
structor. Her world is completely domestic, and throughout the novel
she is seen primarily in terms of the house and garden, sewing, smoking, or daydreaming. Cut off from her mother tongue, she is in one
sense a silent and passive character; meanwhile, Alfredo is seen disci-

plining his unruly students and mentally running through the declensions of the word "rose" in Latin as he sits in an easy chair at home.

Lavínia and Alfredo have a tense relationship, although there is no obvious battle between them. Lavínia commits a few secret acts of rebellion—for example, she shoves a tenderly cared for plant out the window, and later she arranges the knives on the table with their blades turned menacingly inward. Finally, however, her privately expressed unhappiness gives way to a public act of defiance. She momentarily leaves Alfredo, taking a train to the city where she joins another man, Herberto. No details are given about this romantic encounter; all we know is that at some point Lavínia returns on the train and passively resumes her duties in the house. It therefore comes as a surprise when, toward the end of the novel, we discover indirectly that she is dead, having taken an overdose of tranquilizers. (Interestingly, her probable suicide is revealed in the same fragment that discloses Lavínia and Lídia's mother-daughter relationship.) From that moment on, Alfredo insists that the family pictures on the table next to his chair not be disturbed in any way. Their fastidious arrangement allows him to gaze, without any interference or distortion, upon the smiling face of Lavínia in a photo taken many years ago in Paris. The orderliness of the family portraits allows him to feel that in some sense Lavínia is still in the house, maintaining domestic serenity.

The novel calls attention to numerous similarities between Lídia and Lavínia, whose names resemble one another. In the beginning of the book, Lavínia's lover, Herberto, comments on the sound of her name: "Parece um nome de flor. E depois é uma palavra esdrúxula, sobe até um ponto alto e parte-se de repente" (18) (It's like the name of a flower. And after all it is a whimsical name, rising to a high point and suddenly taking off.) Toward the middle of the novel, in a fragment narrated by one of Lídia's former lovers, the following line appears: ". . . Lídia, íris, ígnia, um nome esdrúxulo, que sobe até um ponto fino e alto e se parte de repente, o i quebrado, violado, como uma palavra dita" (48) (Lídia, iris, igneous, a whimsical name, rising to a fine, high point and suddenly taking off, the i broken, violated, like a word spoken.) These nearly identical comments suggest the way in which the women's names are irrevocably linked to the idea of a "sudden taking off," as if there were something unpredictable, indomitable, or unretrieveable about both of them.

The actions of the two women also seem to mirror one another in strange and oblique ways. At a point midway through the book, a fragment ends with a description of Lavínia arriving at the hotel where Herberto is waiting for her: "... sobe no elevador ... bate na porta logo aberta, Herberto abraça-a, beija-a longamente na boca, despe-a devagar. Deitar-se contra o seu corpo" (75) (... she goes up the elevator ... knocks on the door soon opened, Herberto embraces her, kisses her lingeringly on the mouth, undresses her slowly. To lie down against his body). A blank space separates this scene from the next one, which begins: "Subir no elevador, abrir a porta, abraçar Afonso. Ele beija-a longamente na boca, despe-a devagar. Deitar-se contra o seu corpo" (75) (To go up in the elevator, open the door, embrace Afonso. He kisses her lingeringly on the mouth, undresses her slowly. To lie down against his body).

Other, less obvious repetitions are found scattered throughout the book—all of them serve to bind the women closer together. Early in the novel, Lídia is described lying back on the beach, her arm over her head, a straw hat over her eyes, "a luz entrando apesar de tudo através dos orifícios minúsculos, espetando-se nos seus olhos como agulhas" (24) (the light entering in spite of everything through the minute orifices, sticking into her eyes like needles). In a fragment forty pages later, Lídia talks of Lavínia as if she were the mythical Penelope, waiting and knitting to pass the time. Lídia comments: "Um dia voltarei sobre a relva e quando chegar perto tu estarás morta, sentada no banco do jardim, e para castigar-te de sempre teres estado ausente pegarei nas agulhas que seguras ainda, como sempre absorta e fatigada, e espetá-las-ei ternamente nos teus olhos" (65) (Some day I will return over the lawn and when I get close you will be dead, seated on the bench in the garden, and to punish you for having always been absent I will pick up the needles you still hold onto, as always distracted and tired, and I will tenderly stick them in your eyes). In the first of these two passages, there is an association between the light of recognition and pain. Sunning herself on the beach, Lídia is excruciatingly aware of the reality of her situation, which nothing can ease or block out, so that light or truth seems to enter her eyes with blinding force. The second passage, with its image of needles piercing eyes, echoes the first in the sense that it involves both revelation and pain; but whereas Lídia is cognizant of her situation, Lavínia must be made to see—hence Lídia's desire to remove the knitting needles from Lavínia's hand and place them in her eyes.

While the novel emphasizes the affinities between Lídia and Lavínia (so much so that it is often difficult to know which of the two is speaking or is being described), a difference ultimately emerges between the mother and the daughter. Lavínia relies on tranquilizers to help her carry out her duties in the home, but Lídia dumps out the sedatives Afonso gives to her. Also, unlike Lavínia, Lídia constantly resists her "natural" role as homemaker. When she senses that the apartment she and Afonso share is taking on the same ordered appearance of Alcina's house (which she visited once out of curiosity), she pulls out a container of rice, opens it, pours the grains through her fingers, and watches them scatter on the floor. When Afonso installs special security devices on the windows and doors to ensure the safety of their future child, Lídia goes to the hospital where Afonso works and has an abortion. At the end of the novel Lídia walks out of the house and Afonso leans out of the window calling to her to return: "mas a sua voz não podia mais atingí-la" (124) (but his voice could no longer reach her). Lídia is not only "out of reach" but also "abrindo passagem com o corpo" (opening the way with her body), an image which contrasts with Afonso's final act: shutting the window and projecting onto everything about him a mild hatred ("Voltou para dentro e fechou a janela. Havia dentro dele um ódio leve, que se estendia a todas as coisas do mundo" [124]).

I have summarized these events in a much more direct and orderly way than they appear in the text; and I should emphasize that Gersão's whole purpose is to undermine chronology and make rational distinctions seem ambiguous. This technique is important because the novel dramatizes a struggle between men and women rising out of man's desire to impose upon woman a patriarchal domesticity. The struggle on the part of women against order is everywhere present in the novel, as in the repeated images of flight, disruption, disobedience, and in the more explicit acts of resistance, such as abortion and suicide. Quite clearly, the struggle by women against the patriarchy is analogous to the resistance the book displays with regard to the rules and conventions associated with mainstream fiction. The shifting point of view, the disjointed fragments, the vague, ambiguous characterizations, the oblique settings and unorthodox renderings of dialogue and other aspects of voice—all these features of O *Silêncio* problematize the easy logic and clear order of the traditional novel. Thus, the poetic disorder Lídia brings to the house is one with the protean quality Gersão brings to the novel. In effect, both the house women live in and the house of fiction have been presided over by a male, bourgeois culture. As Hélène Cixous notes in "The Laugh of the Medusa," in order for women to "project themselves, to foresee the unforeseeable," all such institutions and codes must be thrown into a certain disarray:

> Women must write through their bodies, they must invent the impregnable language that will wreck partitions, classes, and rhetorics, regulations and codes, they must submerge, cut through, get beyond the ultimate reserve-discourse, including the one that laughs at the very idea of pronouncing the word "silence," the one that, aiming for the impossible, stops short before the word "impossible" and writes it as "the end." (Quoted in *The SIGNS Reader* 1983, 290)

O Silêncio is about this process, and it is therefore deeply concerned with the problem of language, in particular women's struggle against the linguistic norms they receive from the dominant culture. This situation is perhaps best suggested in a scene in which Lavínia is being admonished by Alfredo for not learning Portuguese, which he insists she must learn in order to survive:

> ... é tudo uma questão de contexto, e também de gramática, entrar na norma, seguir a norma, depois tudo é fácil, pode mesmo deixar-se de pensar, tudo surgirá como uma segunda natureza, automático, imediato, como uma resposta preparada para um estímulo já conhecido, a norma substitui-se à ansiedade, oh, essa sua comovente procura das palavras certas, que nunca encontra no momento preciso ... (67–68)

> ... everything is a question of context and of grammar as well, to enter the norm, follow the norm, then everything is easy, you can even stop thinking, everything will come as if it were second nature, automatic, immediate, like a prepared response to a stimulus already known, the norm substitutes anxiety, oh, that touching search of yours for the right words, that you never find when you need them...

But Portugal and Portuguese are foreign to Lavínia, just as, in a more general sense, patriarchy and its language are alien to woman. Lavínia anguishes over this strange culture: "Eu própria não sei mover-me neste mundo estrangeiro de que sempre ignorei a língua, há um código que me falta, uma forma de comunicar, nunca soube exprimir-me e fui sempre arrastada, apenas arrastada pelas palavras de outros" (67) (I myself don't know how to move in this foreign world whose language I always ignored, there's a code that I lack, a form of communicating, I never knew how to express myself and I was always dragged along, merely dragged along by the words of others). One day, after years of pretending to communicate, of being "dragged along," Lavínia lashes out at those around her, shouting over and over:

... algo como inas—inastranka ... uma palavra absurda e louca e perigosa, porque não significava para nós coisa alguma mas tinha certamente sentido noutro código de que não possuíamos a chave, uma palavra inimiga, que estava para além do nosso alcance e nos agredia, nos insultava talvez sem nós sabermos, e outras vezes soava apenas como uma palavra resignada e morta, que não atingia ninguém e não significava coisa alguma, vibrava apenas no silêncio sem mudar nada, sem tocar em nada, uma palavra de vidro, de pedra, solta, isolada, neurótica, arrancada de todas as raízes, uma anémona do mar movendo no vazio os seus muitos braços, os seus cabelos roxos, uma anémona num aquário, por detrás de paredes de vidro. (70-71)

... something like inas—inastranka ... a word that was absurd, crazy and dangerous because it didn't mean anything to us but it certainly had meaning in another code for which we didn't have a key, an enemy word, that was beyond our reach and abused us, insulted us perhaps without our knowing, and other times it sounded merely like a resigned, dead word that didn't reach anyone and didn't mean anything, it merely vibrated in the silence without changing anything, without touching anything, a word made of glass, stone, loose, isolated, neurotic, pulled out from all its roots, a sea anemone moving its many arms and purple hair in the void, an anemone in an aquarium, behind walls made of glass.

As this passage makes clear, the language of silence (or women's language) is "dangerous" because when it is articulated it seems to violate all the rules and all the logic governing reason. However, it is ultimately rendered harmless by "glass walls" or the invisible barriers that keep women contained and silenced.

It is not only women who suffer from this condition. The children in the novel also struggle against a language they are taught in school—a language that is rooted in classical antiquity. Alfredo begins his Portuguese language classes by having his students repeat the Latin forms of certain words. But instead of repeating the declension, "rosa, rosae," the students subvert it by mixing up the letters to produce nonsense constructions such as "asor, sora, sorae." In the end, however, Alfredo wins out over the children by punishing anyone who tries to undermine both the master('s) tongue and its (his) authority.

Although the novel implies that the condition of women is silence, it does not suggest that women are "naturally" voiceless. Instead, it tries to make the silence audible, and it depicts women struggling against authority. Thus Lídia's long monologues disobey in form and content the logic of Afonso's discourse, and her abortion is a tragic act against the paternal order. The novel ends with Lídia "out of reach of Afonso's words" and "walking, opening the way with her body"—two images which suggest that she is no longer being controlled either verbally or physically; rather, like many women in modern Portugal, she is using her body to clear the way for the possibility of her own voice.

APPENDIX

FEMINISM IN PORTUGAL
A Brief History

The recent outpouring of feminist literature in Portugal, including the books discussed in this volume, needs to be understood against the background of a centuries-old tradition of patriarchal law. Perhaps the most convenient place to begin a quick review of this tradition is in the 1500s, when a set of *ordenações* (ordinances) was instituted by the Portuguese monarchy to govern both men and women.[1] An extension of early Roman Law, this highly repressive legislation was designed primarily to keep women subservient, and it was especially rigorous for married women, depriving them of basic human rights. For example, a wife was expected to bow to the authority of her husband in all matters; if she disobeyed, he was allowed to beat her as well as his children and his servants. In the case of adultery, a husband could kill his wife and a father could kill his daughter. (In those few cases in which the killing was deemed unlawful, the maximum penalty imposed on the man was exile for a six-month period—sometimes just to another district.) The husband also controlled the wife's property; if he died or left, the children were declared orphans. If the mother kept the children, which was normally the case, she became their guardian.

The Civil Code introduced in 1867 brought some relief to married women: the wife now shared parental authority over the children and, if the husband died or left, she assumed full legal control. On the whole, however, the Civil Code did very little to improve the situation. Not only did the husband continue to exercise legal control over the wife's property, now he could force his wife back to the home if she left him. Furthermore, although a husband could legally separate from his wife in the case of adultery (divorce was prohibited), a wife could legally separate from her husband only if his mistress was kept in the home or if a gross public scandal or serious mistreatment occurred.

At this time, only men over the age of twenty-one could vote. As early as 1820, an attempt was made to introduce a new law to grant suffrage to a few women. That year, in a session of government, the representative Dr. Borges Barros proposed that mothers with six or more children be given the vote since "ninguém dá mais a um país do que quem lhe dá seus cidadãos" (no one does more for the country than those who give it its citizens) (quoted in Guimarães 1979, 6). Not surprisingly, Barros' proposal fell on deaf ears, and it was never even discussed. While Barros was clearly advocating a kind of biological blackmail, his proposal is historically important: it was the first time the issue of women's voting rights was officially addressed, and it opened the way for future discussion of the topic.

In 1868, the year following the introduction of the Civil Code, a new women's magazine appeared called A Voz Feminina (Woman's Voice). Unlike other women's publications existing at the time, A Voz Feminina was written and edited exclusively by women, and it was the first to show certain radical tendencies. This radicalism was the result of a growing dissatisfaction among women of the middle and upper classes with respect to their situation in Portuguese society. The magazine, which bore the subtitle "a mulher livre ao lado do homem livre" (the free woman beside the free man), encouraged women to liberate themselves through self-education. (The magazine was careful to point out that women should not leave or jeopardize the home in order to achieve their liberation.) By today's standards, A Voz Feminina seems rather tame, but it was considered bold in its time— especially in its call for equality between the sexes. The magazine also represented one of the earliest attempts of a group of women to organize themselves and bring about change. Although it was largely directed toward the middle class, A Voz Feminina raised an important issue for all women, an issue that would become a major theme in the later feminist struggle. As the magazine pointed out quite clearly, in order to secure independence and equality, women must have an adequate education. This was the single most formidable obstacle facing future generations of feminists, especially since the majority of Portuguese women could not read or write.

The Subjection of Women (1869) by John Stuart Mill had a definite impact on the emerging feminism in Portugal. Three years after its appearance, a university professor in Coimbra, José Lopes Praça, published his own treatise entitled A Mulher e a Vida (Woman and Life). In it, Praça demanded that Portuguese women be given access to secondary and university education and that they be permitted to vote (Guimarães 1979, 6). Praça's was only one of several works published in the 1870s and 1880s which discussed the status of women in Portugal. Interestingly, most of the other works were also written by men. It was not until the 1890s that the dominant voice defending women's rights in print was female.

In a general way, the early history of feminism in Portugal is similar to that of the rest of Europe. Although the issue of women's rights was talked about in the early 1800s, it was not until the turn of the century that women began to organize themselves and to call for radical change. Their primary demands were for the vote, educational opportunities, and economic independence. Several women in the forefront during this period deserve special mention, although it is important to note that they did not always agree on the issues.

One of the most prominent early Portuguese feminists was the writer Alice Pestana, who signed her works "Caiel." In addition to writing on topics such as education, maternity, and child care, she advocated the formation of a league of women workers to promote more favorable working conditions. Caiel traveled a great deal, and she wrote newspaper articles on major international feminist events such as the establishment of the International Council of Women in Washington, D.C., in 1888 and the Conference of the League of Women for International Disarmament, held in Paris in 1897. But her passion was writing about the need for educational reform in Portugal. In an essay published in 1892, entitled O Que Deve Ser a Instrução Secundária da Mulher? (What Should Women's Secondary Education Be?), she denounced the Portuguese educational system as archaic, and she demanded improvements be made, especially with regard to women's instruction.[2] In an even more critical study published in 1900, with the rather innocent title Comentários à Vida (Comments

on Life), Caiel continued her attack, citing some startling information regarding the state of education in the country. For example, of
the five million inhabitants in Portugal, only one million or 20 percent were literate. She further pointed out that women constituted
only about one-third of this 20 percent, meaning that less than 7 percent of the female population could read and write (141).

Another early feminist was the philologist and university professor,
Carolina Michaëlis de Vasconcelos, who also spoke out on issues involving women and educational reform. She too traveled outside the
country to attend international feminist conferences, and, in 1896,
she published in a newspaper in Porto a series of enthusiastic articles
based on her experiences at the Feminist congress in Berlin. In 1902,
inspired by what women in other countries were doing to combat illiteracy, she wrote an essay, "O Movimento Feminista em Portugal"
(The Feminist Movement in Portugal), in which she called for the creation of more and better schools for women. Vasconcelos was and still
is considered one of the major figures in Portuguese intellectual life.
Interestingly, however, her reputation in Portugal and abroad is not
based on her feminist activities; rather, she is renowned for having
written extensively on Portuguese literature. In fact, her contribution
to this field was so great that, in 1911, she became the first woman in
Portugal to be appointed to a university chair.

An equally celebrated figure, whose books for young women were
widely read by the middle class, was the novelist and essayist Maria
Amália Vaz de Carvalho. In her books, Carvalho encouraged women
to continue their education even after marriage and children. This
was progressive counseling for the times, since most women all too
readily abandoned their studies as soon as they became wives and
mothers. But Carvalho was not a feminist like her contemporaries
Caiel and Vasconcelos. Like the women of A *Voz Feminina*, Carvalho
felt that a woman's place was in the home. Furthermore, she advised
women to pursue their studies not so much for their own sake as for
that of their husbands. By keeping informed of what was happening in
the world outside, Carvalho felt that wives would be better compan-
ions to their husbands, who were more interested in conversing about
world issues than about routine domestic matters.

Perhaps the two most active members in the early struggle for wom-
en's rights were Ana de Castro Osório, a theoretician who wrote the
first feminist manifesto, *Às Mulheres Portuguesas* (To the Portuguese

Women) (1905); and Adelaide Cabete, a physician, who published widely on issues relating to women's and children's health. In 1909, they founded the Liga Republicana das Mulheres Portuguesas (Republican League of Portuguese Women)—the first organization in Portugal specifically created to defend the rights of women. As part of the Republican party, the league received the support of party leaders such as Bernardino Machado (who later became president of the republic), António José de Almeida, and Magalhães Lima. In return for their support, the league was faithful to Republican ideals.[3] Shortly after its inception, the league issued a proclamation which demanded that the anti-divorce law be repealed, that women be given the vote, and that the 1867 Civil Code be revised, especially with regard to the welfare of women and children. Under the direction of the writer and teacher Maria Veleda, the league immediately launched its own publication entitled A Mulher e a Criança (Woman and Child), which appeared from 1909 to 1914. In 1911, it started another, more radical magazine called A Madrugada (Dawn), which was published until the league disbanded in 1918.

Shortly after the establishment of the republic in 1910, divorce was legalized for both men and women. The new government responded to other demands made by the league by creating a new set of laws called "Leis da Família" (Family Laws). Now adultery carried the same consequences whether committed by a man or a woman; civil marriages were compulsory; and a woman could not be forced back to the home against her will. But the passage of these laws did not fully address all the league's demands. In 1911, the league and women throughout the country suffered a major setback when the Republicans passed a new electoral law which categorically denied women the vote.

The league's anger and frustration that resulted from the passage of this law were momentarily eased by one woman's determination to take advantage of the law's ambiguous wording. In the spring of 1911, Dr. Carolina Beatriz Ângelo set out to register to vote for the upcoming election. A widow and mother, she was over twenty-one, literate, and the head of the household, in other words, she fulfilled all the voting requirements. When she was denied the right to register, she took the case to court and won. On election day, she was cheered by hundreds of women who came from around the country to watch as Ângelo became the first Portuguese woman ever to vote. But this victory was short lived. Not long after, the government changed the law to read that only masculine heads of the household could cast a ballot. The resentment that many women felt toward the Republican party brought about a split within the league. In 1912, Ana de Castro Osório and Carolina Ângelo finally left the league and founded an independent organization called the Associação de Propaganda Feminista (Association of Feminist Propaganda), which concentrated on educational reform.

The year 1914 marked an important new phase in women's emancipation. In that year, Adelaide Cabete founded the Conselho Nacional das Mulheres Portuguesas (National Council of Portuguese Women) which was the most important and longest sustained organization in the history of Portuguese feminism. As the Portuguese branch of the International Women's Council, it brought Portuguese women into contact with women's movements from around the world. Unlike the league, the National Council of Portuguese Women was an independent association which served as the umbrella organization under which all other women's groups in Portugal came together. These included, in addition to the Lisbon-based league and the Association of Feminist Propaganda, the Porto-based Lar da Liga Republicana das Mulheres Portuguesas (Home of the Republican League of Portuguese Women), União das Mulheres Socialistas (Union of Socialist Women), Círculo Feminino Português (Portuguese Women's Circle), and Associação de Costureiras (Association of Seamstresses).

The main objectives of the National Council of Portuguese Women were to defend everything with respect to the bettering of material and moral conditions for women (especially the proletariat), to secure equal pay for equal work, to obtain the vote, and to gain ground in the area of women's legal rights. The council's principal publication was *Alma Feminina* (Woman's Soul) which appeared shortly after the organization got under way. From its inception in 1914 until its demise some thirty years later, *Alma Feminina* informed Portuguese women about national and international feminist activities; it also published special issues on the lives of eminent feminist leaders. The council held two important conferences: the First Portuguese Feminist Congress, which took place in 1924, was attended by some of the highest ranking officials in the government; the second congress, held in 1928, occurred under more difficult conditions owing to the overthrow of the republic and the installation of a right-wing regime. Progovernment newspapers, for example, criticized the convention, claiming it encouraged women to deny their roles as wives and mothers and therefore threatened the sacred institution of the family. But this public condemnation did not alter the fact that the conference was well attended and highly successful. Among those contributing to its success was the law scholar Elina Guimarães, whose work in the area of women's legal rights has made her one of the major figures in the feminist struggle.

As in many other European countries, the First World War brought about an increased participation by Portuguese women in society. In 1917, Ana de Castro Osório founded the Cruzada das Mulheres Portuguesas (Crusade of Portuguese Women), which encouraged women to become active in the war effort. What had the most profound effect on women of this period, however, was the government's call for volunteers to become nurses and to enter the war effort by accompanying the soldiers to France. This caused a major upset in the cultural code of the country and brought about an unprecedented clash between mothers and daughters; the daughters were eager to become active participants in what was happening outside the home instead of assuming the housekeeping role their mothers had inherited.

The postwar years saw a recognition by some countries of women's right to vote (England, 1918; Germany, 1919; and the United States, 1920). In Portugal, women were still denied this basic right even though their service to the country during the war was considerable and had been praised by the government. The council tried to soften the government's hard line on this issue by asking that at least professional women and those with a minimum of a secondary degree be given the vote. Even this modest request was refused. According to more than one historian, this denial was based on the Republican party's belief that women were easily influenced by the church,[4] meaning that they would most likely support the conservative parties that were battling with the Partido Republicano Português (PRP) for control of the government (Robinson 1979, 36; Gallagher 1983, 23). (Ironically, this was precisely why the later fascist government gave women the vote.) Despite this defeat, the early 1920s proved to be one of the most exciting periods of feminist activity in the country. As a result of lobbying by women's groups, coeducation was established in 1920; in addition, more women than ever were obtaining secondary and university degrees and being employed in the school system. However, in 1926, with the installation of the right-wing dictatorship, Portuguese feminism entered one of its most difficult phases.

As in all the totalitarian regimes in Europe, the struggle for women's rights in Portugal was effectively thwarted by Salazar's regime, which came to be known as the *Estado Novo* (New State). The dictator's initial strategy was not to antagonize women's groups, but to praise women if they did what they were told to do and stayed in the home.

The educational advances that women had fought for and partially obtained during the republic were systematically withdrawn by the new regime. Salazar was particularly concerned with controlling the kind of education young women received, and, in 1927, he abolished coeducation in order to make certain that girls would be instructed in areas such as housekeeping and child care. Ten years later, in 1937, he introduced one of many organizations founded to keep women in the home. The Obra das Mães pela Educação Nacional (Work of Mothers for National Education)—whose initials appropriately spelled out OMEN—listed the following as the goals every young woman should pursue: "de ser mulher, saber ciências caseiras, da família, do espírito . . . de criar, educar os futuros homens de Portugal" (to be a wife, to be instructed in matters pertaining to the home, family, and the spirit . . . [and] to raise and educate the future men of Portugal) (quoted in Olim and Marques 1979, 29). Because most of the women in the country were illiterate, the only teachings they could pass on to children were religious ones extolling the virtues of submission and obedience—a situation clearly foreseen by the regime. In order to ensure that women remained confined and that children were kept from being properly educated, the government closed all primary schools, claiming they were an unnecessary luxury. The impact of OMEN on the lives of women and children was devastating to say the very least. Moreover, its oppressive policies remained in effect for thirty years, until the late 1960s, when the organization was finally dismantled.

In 1931, the year in which women in Spain were given the vote, Salazar issued a decree which granted the vote to all women with a secondary degree. (Men had only to be literate.) This was a major gain in the area of women's rights, even though women voters had to pay a special tax and even though the political system in Portugal was such that no choice was offered other than the government's candidates. At the same time Salazar gave a small percentage of women in the country the vote, he passed legislation that worsened the generally repressed condition of women in the nation. For example, the Constitution of 1933 proclaimed that everyone is equal before the law "except, as regards women, the differences resulting from their nature and from the interest of the family" (quoted in *Portugal: Status of Women* 1985, 26). In order to guarantee the safety of the family unit, in 1939, Salazar repealed an earlier law so that now men could force their wives to return to the home if they left.

Although politically Portugal was more aligned with the Axis powers, it managed to remain neutral throughout most of the Second World War. However, in 1943, Salazar allowed the United States to build air bases on the strategic islands of the Azores in the mid-Atlantic. Portugal's belated alliance with the Allies was perceived by many in the Portuguese opposition as a possible turning point in the country's political course. How could Portugal's authoritarian regime not be affected by the wave of liberal democratic principles sweeping over Western Europe? (In 1944, for example, the French government finally gave women the vote, and in 1946, the Italian government followed suit.)

There was, in the early postwar period in Portugal, a short reprieve during which the opposition surprised the government by being better organized than had been anticipated. Women and organizations like the National Council of Portuguese Women were prominent within the opposition, and leaders like Elina Guimarães and the journalist Maria Lamas (who had taken over the leadership of the council and had given it new life by opening its membership to the working class) actively challenged the dictatorship. Because any form of dissent was intolerable to Salazar, he cracked down on the opposition and chose women as one of his targets. In 1946 he repealed the right to vote for married women; a year later, he abolished the council, whose membership had grown to over 2,000. Maria Lamas protested and asked for an explanation for the closure of the council. The government responded by saying that the organization had violated Portuguese law by having the term "National" in its title, and that women did not need an organization anyway, since the government looked out for their welfare. Maria Lamas came under direct attack by the government and was forced out of her job with the magazine for which she had been writing for several years. She went into exile in Paris after having written one of the most important books on women in Portugal, *As Mulheres do Meu País* (The Women of My Country) (1948), and the two-volume *A Mulher no Mundo* (The Woman in the World) (1952).

The 1940s saw the passage of other legislative acts detrimental to the rights and freedom of women in Portugal. Since 1910, civil marriages had been mandatory and divorce had been allowed; however, in 1940, changes were made as a result of the Concordat, an agreement between Portugal and the Vatican which stated that civil ceremonies were no longer compulsory since Catholic weddings had full legal status. Although those married in civil ceremonies could still obtain a divorce, the overwhelming number of marriages were religious, and those united in a Catholic ceremony could not be divorced (Guimarães 1978, 22). As a result, the number of legal and illegal separations rose drastically. Husbands left wives and children, and wives abandoned their homes. The situation became so critical that, in 1950, Salazar passed a law proclaiming that desertion was a crime punishable by imprisonment. And to keep women from straying too far, he instituted a law that prevented married women from obtaining a passport or leaving the country without the notarized permission of their husbands—even if they were separated. This law remained in effect until 1969.

In the late 1950s, the government sanctioned a public program called "casamentos de Santo António" (Saint Anthony's Day weddings), a pernicious ritual celebrating poverty and women's virginity and ensuring more Catholic unions among the masses. As mentioned earlier, religious weddings were popular in Portugal, although not everyone could afford an elaborate church ceremony. In accordance with this new program, the government and local businesses covered all the costs of the wedding, even gifts like vacuum cleaners and pots and pans, for those couples who married in a mass wedding ceremony held on St. Anthony's Day. The only demand placed upon the individual couples was that they provide documented evidence of their poverty and the woman's virginity. Being poor, most of these women had never been to a doctor even when ill, let alone had a routine gynecological exam, which must have frightened more than a few. It was the practice of the government to withhold the names of those applying to be married until after the exam. One might think that this was to spare the woman public embarrassment if she were found not to be "intact"; however, according to an article in the *Diário Popular*, dated 22 April 1958 (the year in which the festivities were officially begun), this secrecy was to protect the reputation and family honor of those future husbands whose future brides did not pass the test.[5] This ritual was extremely popular, as evidenced by newspaper photographs showing dozens of young couples dressed in the finest wedding apparel. Without any change in the requirements, the St. Anthony's Day weddings took place every year until 1973.

The 1960s in Portugal were characterized by strong waves of male emigration due to depressed economic conditions and the desire to avoid the draft as a result of the colonial wars in Africa. Because of the absence of men at home, women in both the rural and urban sectors became more active outside the home. This was not a positive situation for all women, especially for those in the countryside, many of whom were left alone for years struggling to keep their families together.[6] (Even today one can see these "viúvas dos vivos" [widows of the living] working the fields in their traditional black garb which they adopted on the day their husbands left.) It was, however, a particularly liberated time for urban middle-class women, and a considerable number of them became lawyers, doctors, and engineers—professions which in America and England, for example, were almost exclusively held by men.[7]

The Civil Code introduced in 1966 softened some of the restraints on married women. For instance, a married woman could now manage her own money and no longer needed her husband's permission to pursue a profession. (Women had been granted these rights in England at the end of the nineteenth century and in France in 1907.) However, in 1967, a new Civil Code wreaked havoc once more in the area of married women's rights. It stated: "The husband is the head of the family and as such he is to decide and direct on all matters concerning marital life." It further declared that "[i]t is the father, as the head of the household, who directs the children's education, and governs them according to their sex, defends and represents them even before they are born" (quoted in Guimarães 1978, 25).

During a brief liberal period in the late 1960s (when Marcelo Caetano took over after Salazar fell ill), women finally gained the right to vote if they were literate. Organized activities such as the establishment of a work group to oversee women's participation in economic and social life, and conferences, such as the one held in Lisbon on the conditions of women in Portugal, were intermittently allowed. But Caetano's feeble attempts to appease women and other oppositional groups by lifting certain bans merely encouraged the opposition in its struggle to overthrow the regime.

During the dictatorship, women and men worked side by side in organizations like Pragma, a progressive Catholic cooperative, and the Associação do Apoio dos Presos Políticos (Association for the Support of Political Prisoners). In the early 1970s, the physician Isabel do Carmo and her husband Carlos Antunes formed the Partido Revolucionário Proletariado (Revolutionary Proletariat Party) to fight the regime. An extreme leftist organization, its brigades sought to destroy the government through armed actions which included robbing banks and assassinations. It was the only party in the history of Portuguese politics to have a woman as its leader.

Although military men overthrew the regime in 1974, women were responsible for much of the activity that ensued. It is important to remember that, for most of their lives, the majority of women in Portugal rarely left the house, let alone went anywhere unescorted. However, when they learned of the military takeover, they took to the streets and marched along with the soldiers. Women factory workers were especially active; in the textile mills, for example, they were the ones who took over after the owners fled. In a few instances, the women managed to corner the owners before they could escape and kept them imprisoned in the mills for days. Women also led many of the strikes that took place at this time (strikes were illegal during the dictatorship), and several of the newly formed unions had women in their leadership. Poor and working-class housewives also took an active role in dismantling the institutions fostered by the regime. They immediately seized homes that had been standing vacant for years and moved their families out of the slums and into decent accommodations. Women of all social classes banded together to take over schools and public service operations, and they formed commissions to plan new housing projects and public works cooperatives. In addition, they appeared on radio and television—the first time in the history of the country that women's voices had been clearly heard.[8] Women of the feminist group Movimento da Libertação da Mulher (Women's Liberation Movement) held a rally in the center of Lisbon. There they issued proclamations denouncing the oppressed condition of women in the country, and they scandalized onlookers by burning their brooms and bras, the symbols of their oppression.[9]

The establishment of the democracy in Portugal brought into effect new laws, which significantly improved the lot of women as well as men in the country. In 1975, divorce was made possible for all those with church marriages; that same year, the Comissão para a Política Social Relativa à Mulher (Commission for Social Politics Relative to Women), established in 1973, was renamed the Comissão da Condição Feminina (Commission on the Status of Women) and was made part of the Ministry of Social Affairs. The purpose of this organization (now attached to the Office of the Prime Minister) is to protect women's rights and to work toward improving the attitudes of both men and women with regard to reform. Over the last ten years, it has played an active role in the creation of important legislation for women, such as the ninety-day maternity act, and in the revision of older laws, such as the penal code, to ensure that women's rights are being upheld. The commission also sponsors seminars on women-related topics, and, in the early 1980s, it officially launched women's studies in Portuguese university life.

The recent history of Portugal has seen a good many other important manifestations of the feminist struggle. The Constitution of 1976 states that men and women are equal, and it forbids any form of discrimination. The constitution also amended the Civil Code so that the wife is equal to the husband in all aspects of marital and family life. Since the revolution, a number of nongovernmental organizations have come forward (some formed recently, others having operated clandestinely during the regime) to help oversee women's rights and representation in all aspects of daily life. Among the independent groups are the Liga dos Direitos das Mulheres (Women's Rights League), the Intervenção Feminina (Women's Intervention), the Graal (Grail), the Comité de Mulheres Trabalhadoras (Committee of Women Workers), and the Cooperativa Editora das Mulheres (Editorial Cooperative of Women). Various other women's groups are also directly or indirectly supported by political parties, such as the Mulheres Socialistas (Socialist Women), the Mulheres Portuguesas Sociais Democráticas (Portuguese Social Democratic Women), and the Movimento Democrático de Mulheres (Women's Democratic Movement), which is the largest women's group in the country with a membership of approximately 12,000.

Although the early postrevolutionary period (1974–1978) saw intense political activity on the part of feminists and other women's
groups, in the subsequent years, as the consolidation process got
under way, women found themselves relegated to the sidelines. Their
political activity no longer needed, women were expected to return to
their homes and resume their duties as wives and mothers, leaving the
running of the country to the men. As a result, few women were
elected to roles of leadership in the government. This was particularly
disconcerting to women, given the fact that they constituted between
21 percent and 46 percent of the membership of the different political
parties represented in the parliament (*Portugal* 1985, 39). There was a
brief banner period when Maria de Lourdes Pintasilgo was appointed
prime minister in 1979. During her short term in office, she and other
women in the government worked toward major reforms. Among the
accomplishments of that period was the establishment of the
Comissão para a Igualdade do Trabalho e Emprego (Commission for
Equality in Work and Employment). But since then, and particularly
in the last several years, women's representation in the government
has continued to decrease, and there is no indication that the situation is likely to change in the near future. It is important to add here
that, as a direct result of their low political representation, women are
suffering tremendously in the economic sphere. Not only do women
constitute about 70 percent of the unemployed (Gomes 1986, 94),
but they are also regularly discriminated against in the work place with
respect to the quality of job and salary.

Although women have not fared well in the political and economic
arenas, they have made considerable progress in the private and social
services sectors where their representation is more in evidence. (Almost all the women holding major government positions have been
elected to serve in the areas of education, health and welfare, and
other social programs, which are traditionally associated with
women.) Family planning centers were opened in 1976, and sex education was made mandatory by law. Child care centers and shelters for
abused women are growing in numbers, and nationwide literacy programs are in effect. Nevertheless, illiteracy among women is still a
major obstacle to the success of the women's rights struggle. According to a 1981 survey, 23 percent of the women over ten years of age
could not read or write (*Portugal* 1985, 53). One of the main objectives of organizations like the Commission on the Status of Women

and Grail is to educate women, especially in the rural areas where illiteracy is widespread. These groups not only teach women to read and write, but they also instruct them in basic health care. Most important, they try to raise the consciousness of women by instilling within them a sense of their importance in the communities where they live and work.[10] According to Bertina Sousa Gomes, a central figure in the commission, in order to achieve real change, it is first necessary to educate thousands of women. Gomes makes it quite clear that, as long as so much of the female population is still lacking a general awareness of its condition, any declaration of a full-scale "women's movement" in Portugal is premature.[11]

On the level of literary culture, the situation looks far better. An important recent phenomenon, promoting increased interaction and awareness among women, is the creation of "Espaços"—spaces for the exhibition of women's works in literature and the arts and for lectures on women-related topics. Within the last few years, two have been launched: one in Lisbon by the magazine *Mulheres* (Women) at the headquarters of the Movimento Democrático de Mulheres, and the other in Costa da Caparica, by the novelist Maria Isabel Barreno. The five texts discussed in the previous chapters are obviously connected to these and other developments. In literature at least, as I have tried to show, the achievement of Portuguese women has been spectacular, producing books that compare favorably with any in modern Europe.

NOTES

1. I found much of the early historical information given here in books, pamphlets, and other materials published by the Commission on the Status of Women in Lisbon. An especially helpful booklet was Elina Guimarães' *Portuguese Women Past and Present* (1978). (In 1979, a slightly different version of this work was published in Portuguese under the title *Mulheres Portuguesas Ontem e Hoje.*) Equally invaluable was Regina Tavares da Silva's *Feminismo em Portugal: Na Voz de Mulheres Escritoras do Início do Séc. XX.* (Feminism in Portugal: In the Voice of Women Writers from the Beginning of the Twentieth Century) (1982).

2. According to Elina Guimarães, the educational situation in Portugal at the turn of the century was extremely bad:

Working-class girls got no education at all. Middle- and upper-class ones were not much better off. At school or at home they learned a smattering of foreign languages, embroidery, and especially the piano. In the eighties, out of more than two hundred pupils in a girls' school only two did not play the piano. One had a heart condition and the other a father—a leading University professor—who saw no point in teaching music to a girl who did not like it. He was greatly blamed and very much criticised. (1978, 14).

3. It should be noted here that, during the early 1900s, the Republicans sought as much public support as possible in their campaign to overthrow the monarchy. Although the league was organized by women for the protection of women's rights, it was created within and fostered by an all-male political party which saw it as a way to politicize large numbers of women and gain their support. At a meeting held in Setúbal in 1909, the Republican party promised that, once in power, it would grant women social and political equality. In its initial phase, then, the league promoted the programs of the party, and the Republicans praised the league for its work. However, not long after the republic became a reality, the league became less Republican and more women-oriented, largely because the party failed to carry out all its promises.

4. The Partido Republicano Português (PRP), the largest party in the government, was in control throughout most of the years of the republic. It was also fervently anticlerical.

5. This article including photographs is included in Leonor Nunes' "Que Bonitos Eram os Casamentos de Santo António" (How Pretty the St. Anthony's Day Weddings Were) (1987).

6. For a detailed account of these matriarchal societies in the interior, consult Caroline B. Brettell, *Men Who Migrate, Women Who Wait* (1986).

7. In her book *O Falso Neutro: Um Estudo Sobre a Discriminação Sexual no Ensino* (The False Neuter: A Study on Sexual Discrimination in Teaching) (1986), Maria Isabel Barreno points out that, unlike most Western societies, Portugal had a significant number of women entering the fields of science and industry in the 1950s and 1960s. Her theory is that because there never was a strong middle class in Portugal, young women were not instilled with the typically bourgeois notion that certain areas of study were "male." (See pages 39–40.)

8. In 1975, the Commission on the Status of Women in Lisbon sponsored a teleforum which caused a minor sensation. Not only did it feature women of the middle class speaking out against repression, but it also included a working-class woman, who came to the forum in her bare feet to denounce the treatment women received in the factories.

9. The MLM was severely criticized by both men and women for its "crude" acts. By 1976, the group no longer existed. To this day the word "feminist" in Portugal is associated with the MLM and its unforgettable rally; this

is, in part, why most women and women's organizations in the country do not call themselves feminist.

10. For an account of one of these programs, which took place in the village of Fareginhas in northern Portugal, see Teresa Joaquim, *Mulheres de uma Aldeia* (Women of a Village) (1985).

11. Interview in Lisbon on May 26, 1987. Also, see her "Doze Anos de Democracia em Portugal: O Papel das Mulheres" (Twelve Years of Democracy in Portugal: The Role of Women) (1986).

BIBLIOGRAPHY

Alcoforado, Mariana. *Lettres Portugaises*. Paris: Garnier Frères, 1962.

Bakhtin, Mikhail. *Rabelais and His World*. Translated by Helen Iswolsky. Bloomington: Indiana University Press, 1984.

Balsemão, Francisco Pinto. "The Constitution and Politics: Options for the Future." In *Portugal in the 1980s: Dilemmas of Democratic Consolidation*, edited by Kenneth Maxwell. Westport, Conn.: Greenwood Press, 1986. 197–232.

Barreno, Maria Isabel. *O Falso Neutro: Um Estudo Sobre a Discriminação Sexual no Ensino*. Lisbon: Instituto de Estudos Para o Desenvolvimento, 1986.

Barreno, Maria Isabel, et al. *Fantástico no Feminino*. Lisbon: Editora Rolim, 1985.

Barreno, Maria Isabel, Maria Teresa Horta, and Maria Velho da Costa. *Novas Cartas Portuguesas*. Lisbon: Estúdios Cor, 1972.

――― , *The Three Marias: New Portuguese Letters*. Translated by Helen R. Lane. New York: Doubleday and Co., Inc., 1975.

Botelho, Fernanda. *O Ângulo Raso*. Lisbon: Livraria Bertrand, 1957.

―――. *Calendário Privado*. Lisbon: Livraria Bertrand, 1958.

―――. *As Coordenadas Líricas*. Lisbon: Távola Redonda, 1956.

―――. *O Enigma das Sete Alíneas*. Lisbon: Graal, 1951.

―――. *Esta Noite Sonhei com Brueghel*. Lisbon: Contexto, 1987.

_____ A Gata e a Fábula. Lisbon: Livraria Bertrand, 1960.

_____. Lourenço é Nome de Jogral. Lisbon: Livraria Bertrand, 1971.

_____. Terra Sem Música. Lisbon: Livraria Bertrand, 1969.

_____. Xerazade e os Outros: Romance (Tragédia em Forma de). Lisbon: Livraria Bertrand, 1964.

Brandão, Ignácio de Loyola. Zero: Romance Pré-Histórico. Rio de Janeiro: Editora Brasília, 1975.

Brettell, Caroline B. Men Who Migrate, Women Who Wait. Princeton, N.J.: Princeton University Press, 1986.

Brontë, Charlotte. Jane Eyre. New York: Dodd, Mead, 1944.

Brontë, Emily. Wuthering Heights. Oxford: Clarendon Press, 1976.

Bruneau, Thomas C., and Alex Macleod. Politics in Contemporary Portugal: Parties and the Consolidation of Democracy. Boulder, Colo.: Lynne Rienner Publishers, 1986.

Caiel [Alice Pestana]. Comentários à Vida. Lisbon: António Maria Pereira, 1900.

_____. O Que Deve Ser a Instrução Secundária da Mulher? Lisbon: Typographia e Stereotypia Moderna, 1892.

Carmo, José Palla e. "Literatura e 'literariedade': Xerazade e os Outros de Fernanda Botelho." In Do Livro à Leitura. Lisbon: Publicações Europa-América, 1971. 119–30.

Chopin, Kate. The Awakening. New York: Bantam Classic, 1981.

Cixous, Hélène. "The Laugh of the Medusa." Translated by Keith Cohen and Paula Cohen. In The SIGNS Reader, edited by Elizabeth Abel and Emily K. Abel. Chicago: University of Chicago Press, 1983. 279–97.

Correia, Hélia. 1983. Montedemo. 2d ed. Lisbon: Ulmeiro, 1984.

_____. O Número dos Vivos. Lisbon: Relógio d'Água, 1982.

_____. 1981. O Separar das Águas. 2d ed. Lisbon: Ulmeiro, 1985.

Davis, Lennard J. Resisting Novels. New York: Methuen, 1987.

Fleenor, Juliann E., ed. The Female Gothic. Montreal: Eden Press, 1983.

Fonseca, Mary Lyndon. "The Case of the Three Marias." Ms. Magazine 3 (January 1975): 84–85, 108.

Gallagher, Tom. Portugal: A Twentieth-Century Interpretation. Manchester, England: Manchester University Press, 1983.

Garnier, Christine. Salazar: An Intimate Portrait. Translated from the French. New York: Farrar, Straus, and Young, 1954.

Gersão, Teolinda. 1981. O Silêncio. 3d ed. Lisbon: O Jornal, 1984.

Gomes, Bertina Sousa. "Doze Anos de Democracia em Portugal: O Papel das Mulheres." Desenvolvimento Ano III, no. 3 (Outubro 1986): 87–96.

Guimarães, Elina. Mulheres Portuguesas Ontem e Hoje. Lisbon: Comissão da Condição Feminina, 1979.

_____. *Portuguese Women Past and Present*. Lisbon: Comissão da Condição Feminina, 1978.

Joaquim, Teresa. *Mulheres de uma Aldeia*. Lisbon: Ulmeiro/Fémina, 1985.

Jorge, Lídia. *O Cais das Merendas*. Lisbon: Publicações Europa-América, 1982.

_____. *A Costa dos Murmúrios*. Lisbon: Publicações Dom Quixote, 1988.

_____. 1980. *O Dia dos Prodígios*. 4th ed. Lisbon: Publicações Europa-América, 1982.

_____. *Notícia da Cidade Silvestre*. Lisbon: Publicações Europa-América, 1984.

_____. Public lecture at the Universidade de Lisboa. Lisbon: 14 March 1986.

Lamas, Maria. *A Mulher no Mundo*. 2 vols. Lisbon: Editora da Casa do Estudante do Brasil, 1952.

_____. *As Mulheres do Meu País*. Lisbon: Actualis Lda., 1948.

Lispector, Clarice. *Perto do Coração Selvagem*. 2d. ed. São Paulo: Livraria Francisco Alves, 1963.

McCullers, Carson. *The Ballad of the Sad Café: The Novels and Stories of Carson McCullers*. Boston: Houghton Mifflin, 1951.

Magalhães, Isabel Allegro de. *O Tempo das Mulheres: A Dimensão Temporal na Escrita Feminina Contemporânea*. Lisbon: Imprensa Nacional—Casa da Moeda, 1987.

Maurier, Daphne du. *Rebecca*. New York: Doubleday and Co., 1938.

Maxwell, Kenneth. "At the Crossroads." In *Portugal in the 1980s: Dilemmas of Democratic Consolidation*. Boulder, Colo.: Lynne Rienner Publishers, 1986. 4–15.

Mendonça, Fernando. "As Relações Humanas e os Mitos da Profundidade." In *O Romance Português Contemporâneo: 1930–1964*. São Paulo: Faculdade de Filosofia, Ciências e Letras de Assis, 1966. 159–63.

_____. "Ficção de Autoria Feminina ou o Sabor da Solidão." In *A Literatura Portuguesa do Século XX*. São Paulo: HUCITEC. 1973. 172–94.

Mill, John Stuart. *The Subjection of Women*. Cambridge, Mass.: MIT Press, 1970.

Moers, Ellen. *Literary Women*. New York: Doubleday and Co., Inc., 1976.

Moniz Egas. *A Vida Sexual: Fisiologia e Pathologia*. 5th ed. Lisbon: Casa Ventura Abrantes, 1922.

Nunes, Leonor. "Que Bonitos Eram os Casamentos de Santo António." *Mulheres* 110 (Junho 1987): 14–17.

Olim, Ivone, and Margarida Marques. *Luta de Mulheres pelo Voto*. Lisbon: Editora das Mulheres, 1979.

Osório, Ana de Castro. *Às Mulheres Portuguesas*. Lisbon: Livraria Editora Viúva Tavares Cardoso, 1905.

Perry, Ruth. *Letters, Women, and the Novel*. New York: AMS Press, Inc., 1980.

Poppe, Manuel. "Literatura e o Absurdo—*Xerazade e os Outros*." In *Temas de*

Literature Viva: 35 Escritores Contemporâneos. Lisbon: Imprensa Nacional, 1982. 115–19.

Portugal: Status of Women. 4th ed. Lisbon: Commission on the Status of Women, 1985.

Praça, José Lopes. *A Mulher e a Vida ou a Mulher Considerada Debaixo dos Seus Principais.* Coimbra: Imprensa da Universidade, 1872.

Rebelo, Maria da Glória Martins. "Fernanda Botelho: A Literatura como Matéria Romanesca." *Suplemento Literário: Minas Gerais* 597 (11 March 1978): 67; 599 (25 March 1978): 6–7.

Regency, Barbara Hill. *Madness and Sexual Politics in the Feminist Novel.* Madison: University of Wisconsin Press, 1978.

Ribeiro, Maria Aparecida. "A Origem da Estrutura Trágica de *Xerazade e os Outros.*" *Colóquio* 36 (1977): 39–44.

Robinson, Richard A. H. *Contemporary Portugal.* London: George Allen and Unwin, 1979.

Rosa, João Guimarães. "Cara de Bronze." In *No Urubùquaquá, no Pinhém.* 4th ed. Rio: Livraria José Olympio Editora, 1969. 73–127.

Salazar, António de Oliveira. *Doctrine and Action.* Translated by Robert Broughton. London: Faber and Faber, 1939.

Sena, Jorge de. *O Físico Prodigioso.* 2d. ed. Lisbon: Edições 70, 1979.

Shelley, Mary. *Frankenstein.* London: Penguin, 1988.

Silva, Regina Tavares da. *Feminismo em Portugal: Na Voz de Mulheres Escritoras do Início do Sec. XX.* Lisbon: Comisão da Condição Feminina, 1982.

Vasconcelos, Carolina Michaëlis de. "O Congresso Feminista em Berlin." *O Comércio do Porto* (19, 21, 25, 26, 27 Novembro 1896).

———. "O Movimento Feminista em Portugal." *O Primeiro de Janeiro* (Porto) (11, 12, 13, 14, 16, 18 Setembro 1902).

Wheeler, Douglas. *Republican Portugal: A Political History (1910–1926).* Madison: University of Wisconsin Press, 1978.

Williams, Raymond. *Culture.* Great Britain: Fontana, 1981.

Woolf, Virginia. *Between the Acts.* 1941. London: The Hogarth Press, 1969.

———. *Collected Essays III.* 1925. London: The Hogarth Press, 1967.

———. *A Room of One's Own.* 1929. London: The Hogarth Press, 1967.

———. *The Voyage Out.* 1915. London: The Hogarth Press, 1965.

———. *The Waves.* 1931. London: The Hogarth Press, 1963.

INDEX

Address, modes of, 62, 66, 72 n.7, 98
Adultery, 13, 114, 117
Africa, 56, 65, 66, 69, 92 n.6. See
    also Wars in Africa
Alcoforado, Mariana, 5, 6, 9, 10,
    14, 18
Algarve, xv, 50, 51, 62, 70, 71, 75
Allied powers, 121
Alma Feminina (Woman's Soul), 118
Almeida, António José de, 117
Ambas as Mãos sobre o Corpo
    (Both Hands over Her Body), 5
America, 4, 23 n.1, 123
Ângelo, Dr. Carolina Beatriz, 117,
    118
Anticlericalism, 69, 128 n.4
Antunes, António Lobo, 72 n.1
Antunes, Carlos, 124
As Mulheres Portuguesas (To the
    Portuguese Women), 116

Associação de Costureiras (Associ-
    ation of Seamstresses), 118
Associação de Propaganda
    Feminista (Association of Femi-
    nist Propaganda), 118
Associação do Apoio dos Presos
    Políticos (Association for the
    Support of Political Prisoners),
    124
Authorial voice, 35, 47
The Awakening, 36, 47
Axis powers, 121
Azores, 121

Bakhtin, Mikhail, 55, 72 n.4
The Ballad of the Sad Café, 92 n.5
Balsemão, Francisco Pinto, 69
Barreno, Maria Isabel, xiii, 1–23,
    92 n.1, 127, 128 n.7
Barros, Dr. Borges, 114

Bessa-Luís, Agustina, xiii, xvi
Between the Acts, 97
Bildungsroman, 21
"Bodily lower stratum," 55
Botelho, Fernanda, xiii, 25–48
Bourgeois culture, 27, 75
Bourgeois realism, 13
Bouton, Noël, 5, 6, 9, 15, 18
Braga, Maria Ondina, 92 n.1
Branco, Camilo Castelo, 76
Brandão, Ignácio de Loyola, 72 n.3
Brazil, 68. See also *Telenovela*
Brettell, Caroline B., 128 n.6
Brontës, 76
Bruneau, Thomas C., 69

Cabete, Adelaide, 117, 118
Caetano, Marcelo, 2, 4, 25, 68,
    123–24
Caiel (Alice Pestana), 115–16
O Cais das Merendas (Picnic
    Quay), 71, 72 n.1, 86
"Cara de Bronze" (Bronze Face),
    72 n.3
Carmo, Isabel do, 124
Carmo, José Palla e, 48 n.1, n.3
Carpinteiro, Margarida, xiii
Carvalho, Maria Amália Vaz de, 116
"Casamentos de Santo António"
    (St. Anthony's Day weddings),
    122–23, 128 n.5
Catholic church, 3, 119
Cause and effect, 29, 30, 58
Censorship, 6, 90
Child care, 115, 126
Chopin, Kate, 36, 47
Círculo Feminino Português (Por-
    tuguese Women's Circle), 118
Civil Code, 113–14, 117, 123, 125
Cixous, Hélène, 110
Closure, 22, 29, 47
Colonialism, 6, 72 n.4, 92 n.6

Comentários à Vida (Comments on
    Life), 115
Comissão da Condição Feminina
    (Commission on the Status of
    Women), 125, 126–27, 127 n.1,
    128 n.8
Comissão para a Igualdade do
    Trabalho e Emprego (Commis-
    sion for Equality in Work and
    Employment), 126
Comissão para a Política Social
    Relativa à Mulher (Commission
    for Social Politics Relative to
    Women), 125
Comité das Mulheres Traba-
    lhadoras (Committee of Women
    Workers), 125
Concordat, 122
Conselho Nacional das Mulheres
    Portuguesas (National Council
    of Portuguese Women), 118–19,
    121
Constitution, 69, 121, 125
Convent, 5, 15, 16, 17, 18
Conventions of narrative realism,
    35, 49, 62, 67, 109
Cooperativa Editora das Mulheres
    (Editorial Cooperative of
    Women), 125
Correia, Clara Pinto, xiii, 92 n.1
Correia, Hélia, xiii, 75–93
Correia, Natália, xiii, 6
A Costa dos Murmúrios (The
    Coast of Murmurs), 72 n.1
"Crazy Jane," 83
Cruzada das Mulheres Portuguesas
    (Crusade of Portuguese
    Women), 119
Cultural dynamizing, 69

Davis, Lennard J., 72 n.5
Decentered text, 16, 22, 31, 51, 62

Decolonization, 68, 69
Democracy in Portugal, xvi, 8, 68, 72-73 n.8, 91, 125, 129 n.11
De Noite as Árvores São Negras (By Night the Trees Are Black), 5
O Dia dos Prodígios (The Day of Wonders), 49-73, 79
Dialogue, 34, 52, 58, 62, 94, 95-104, 109. *See also* Quotation; Speech
Diário Popular, 123
Dictatorship in Portugal, xiv, 25, 47, 68, 90, 91, 120. *See also* Caetano, Marcelo; Regime; Salazar, Antonio de Oliveira
Dictionary of Witchcraft, 13
Dinesen, Isak, 26
Divorce, 114, 117, 122, 125
Domesticity, xv, 78-79, 104, 106, 109
Dominant culture, xvi, 21, 110

Emigration, 6, 123, 128 n.6
England, 4, 8, 70, 76, 94, 119, 123
Epic, 54, 61, 63, 65, 68
Epistolary form, 9, 10, 14, 15, 16, 19. *See also* Epistolary narrative; Letters
Epistolary narrative, 9. *See also* Epistolary form; Letters
Eroticism, 4, 10, 81-82, 86, 90, 91
Estado Novo (New State), 120. *See also* Dictatorship; Regime; Salazar, Antonio de Oliveira
Estrangement, xvi, 28, 50, 58, 75, 77

Family, 2, 3, 78, 92 n.3, 119, 120, 121, 123, 125
Family planning, 69, 126
Fantastic, 51, 58, 75, 76, 77, 82, 96
Faulkner, William, 50

Feminism in Portugal, xiv, 26, 91, 113-29
Feminist literature, 25, 26, 36, 77, 79, 113
Feminist movement in Portugal, 21, 129
O Físico Prodigioso (The Wondrous Physician), 72 n.6
Folklore, 50, 52, 53, 75, 80, 91
Fonseca, Mary Lyndon, 23 n.1
Fragmentation, 9, 25, 30, 97-98, 100
France, 70, 121, 123
Frankenstein, 76, 89
Freud, Sigmund, 75, 76

Gallagher, Tom, 4, 69, 119
Garnier, Christine, 3, 4, 8
Gender, 28, 29
Genre, 5, 8, 76, 92 n.1
Germany, 70
Gersão, Teolinda, xiii, 72 n.1, 93-112
Gomes, Bertina Sousa, 127, 129 n.11
Gomes, Luísa Costa, xiii, 92 n.1
Gonçalves, Olga, xiii, 72 n.1, 92 n.1
Gothic conventions, 75-77, 78, 79, 81, 82, 89, 91, 92 n.4
Guilleragues, 5
Guimarães, Elina, 114, 115, 119, 121, 122, 123, 127 n.1
Graal (Grail), 125, 126-27

Horta, Maria Teresa, xiii, 1-23, 71 n.1, 92 n.1

Ideology, xiv, xvi, 1, 25, 49, 58
Intertextuality, 15
Intervenção Feminina (Women's Intervention), 125

Irony, 50, 51, 53, 69, 71, 76, 77,
    91, 97. *See also* Satire
Italy, 21

Jane Eyre, 76, 92 n.4
Jorge, Lídia, xiii, xv, 49–73, 75, 79,
    86, 91

Laing, R. D., 92 n.3
Lamas, Maria, 121–22
Lane, Helen R., 1, 9, 20, 22, 23 n.1
Lar da Liga Republicana das
    Mulheres Portuguesas (Home of
    the Republican League of Portu-
    guese Women), 118
"The Laugh of the Medusa," 110
"Leis da Família" (Family Laws), 117
Letters, 5, 6, 7, 9, 14, 15, 17, 18,
    19–21, 23 n.3. *See also* Episto-
    lary form; Epistolary narrative
Lettres Portugaises, 5, 14–18
Liga dos Direitos das Mulheres
    (Women's Rights League), 125
Liga Republicana das Mulheres
    Portuguesas (Republican League
    of Portuguese Women), 117,
    118
Lima, Magalhães, 117
Linearity, 14, 22, 28, 58, 61, 62,
    97. *See also* Nonlinearity
Lispector, Clarice, 93
Literacy, 116, 120, 123, 126
Llansol, Maria Gabriela, xiii
Louro, Maria Regina, xiii, 92 n.1

McCullers, Carson, 92 n.5
Machado, Bernardino, 117
Macleod, Alex, 69
Madness, 77, 79, 82–83, 92 n.4.
    See also Gothic conventions
A Madrugada (Dawn), 117
Magical realism, 51, 71, 80

Maina Mendes, 5
Marriage in Portugal, 122, 125. *See
    also* "Casamentos de Santo
    António"
Marques, Margarida, 120
Márquez, Gabriel García, 51
Maternity, 79, 89, 115
Maternity act, 125
Maurier, Daphne du, 76
Maxwell, Kenneth, 69
*Men Who Migrate, Women Who
    Wait,* 127 n.6
Middle Ages, 96
Militarism, xv
Military in Portugal, 7, 68, 124
Mill, John Stuart, 115
Minha Senhora de Mim (Milady of
    Me), 4, 5
Mise-en-abyme, 96
Mise-en-scène, 76
Modernism, xvi, 13, 25, 26, 27, 98.
    See also Montage
Modernity, 49, 68, 91
Moers, Ellen, 92 n.2
Monarchy in Portugal, 52–53, 113,
    128 n.3
Moniz, Egas, 91
Montage, xv, 9. *See also*
    Modernism
Montedemo (Devil Mountain),
    75–93
Movimento da Libertação da
    Mulher (Women's Liberation
    Movement), 124–25, 128–29 n.9
Movimento Democrático de
    Mulheres (Women's Democratic
    Movement), 125, 127
"O Movimento Feminista em Por-
    tugal" (The Feminist Movement
    in Portugal), 115
A Mulher e a Criança (Woman and
    Child), 117

A Mulher e a Vida (Woman and Life), 115
A Mulher no Mundo (The Woman in the World), 122
Mulheres (Women), 127
As Mulheres do Meu País (The Women of My Country), 122
Mulheres Portuguesas Sociais Democráticas (Portuguese Social Democratic Women), 125
Mulheres Socialistas (Socialist Women), 125
Myth, 25, 26, 46, 54, 75

Narration, 56, 64, 67, 80, 82, 98
Narrative form, xv, 7–8, 9, 15, 21, 22, 26–28, 29, 31, 34, 50, 57, 58, 62, 68, 71, 97, 109
National identity in Portugal, 70, 71
Nonlinearity, 14, 28, 62. *See also* Linearity
Notícias da Cidade Silvestre (News from the Sylvan City), 72 n.1
Novas Cartas Portuguesas, 1–23, 25, 27, 91
Novelistic form, 8, 9, 14, 25–28, 49, 53, 58, 61, 62, 109–10. *See also* Realism
O Número dos Vivos (The Number of the Living), 77, 78, 85

Obra das Mães pela Educação Nacional (Work of Mothers for National Education), 120
Olim, Ivone, 120
Opposition in Portugal, 121, 124
Oppression, xv, 20, 21, 26, 40, 41, 44, 79, 113–29. *See also* Repression
Oral culture, 50, 62. *See also* Oratory

Oratory, 65, 66, 68. *See also* Oral culture
Ordenações (Ordinances), 113
Organic unity, 13
Osborne, Dorothy, 23 n.3
Os Outros Legítimos Superiores (The Other Legitimate Superior Ones), 5

Parabasis, 48 n.4
Partido Republicano Português (Portuguese Republican Party), 119, 128 n.4
Partido Revolucionário Proletariado (Revolutionary Proletariat Party), 124. *See also* Antunes, Carlos; Carmo, Isabel do
Patriarchy, xiv, 18, 22, 25, 35, 65, 75, 91, 109, 110, 113
Penelope, myth of, 54, 108
Perry, Ruth, 17, 19, 23 nn.4, 5
Perto do Coração Selvagem (Close to the Savage Heart), 93
Pestana, Alice, 115–16
Pintasilgo, Maria de Lourdes, 126
Plancy, Collin de, 13
Point of view, 10, 26, 30, 31, 34, 35, 97–98
Polyphonic writing, xv, 16, 22, 62
Portugal: Status of Women, 121, 126
Portuguese Penal Code, 13, 125
Portuguese Women Past and Present, 127 n.1
Postmodernism, xvi, 35
Praça, José Lopes, 115
Pragma, 124
Presentational rhetoric, 62, 66, 67, 72 n.7
Punctuation, 100, 102

O Que Deve Ser a Instrução Secundária da Mulher? (What

Should Women's Secondary Instruction Be?), 115
Quotation, 99, 100. *See also* Dialogue; Speech

Racism, 88
Realism, xvi, 8, 14, 16, 22, 27, 31, 51, 58, 65, 96
Rebecca, 76
Regime, 1, 2, 53, 68, 119, 120–24. *See also* Dictatorship
Representation, xiv, 8, 28, 71
Representational techniques, 49, 58
Repression, 18, 75–76. *See also* Oppression
Republican party in Portugal, 117–18, 128 n.3. *See also* Partido Republicano Português
Republic of Portugal, 52, 73 n.8, 117, 119, 128 n.3
Retornados (Returnees), 69, 88, 92 n.6
Revolution in Portugal, xiii, 2, 25, 49, 50, 53, 56, 57, 61, 62, 68, 69, 71, 72 n.4, 88, 91
Richardson, Samuel, 14
Robinson, Richard A. H., 69, 91, 119
A Room of One's Own, 1, 8, 27
Rosa, João Guimarães, 72 n.3
Rulfo, Juan, 51
Run-on sentences, 99

Salazar, António de Oliveira, xiv, 2, 3, 4, 25, 68, 72 n.4, 90, 120–21, 123. *See also* Dictatorship; Regime
Saramago, José, 72 n.1
Satire, 51, 69, 75, 76, 80, 85, 91. *See also* Irony
Scheherazade, 25–27, 36, 45, 46
Sena, Jorge de, 72 n.6

O Separar das Águas (The Parting of the Waters), 77
Sexism, 90. *See also* Sexual themes
Sexual themes, 10, 75–93
Shelley, Mary, 76, 89
Silence, 15, 25, 31, 61, 62, 93–112
O Silêncio, 93–112
Simultaneity, 28, 31, 33–34
South Africa, 68
Spain, 68, 69
Speech, representation of, 51, 58–68, 71, 72 n.3, 94–104, 110, 112. *See also* Dialogue; Quotation
Storytelling, 26, 27, 30, 46, 51, 56, 57–58, 63, 66–67
Stream of consciousness, 99
Strikes, 124
The Subjection of Women, 115
Supernatural, 51, 53, 55, 75, 77, 81, 82

Telenovela, 70
Tomar, 69
The Three Marias, 1–23, 25, 91; arrest and trial of, 6, 7, 91
Tragedy, 8, 26–28, 41, 46, 47
Typography, 51, 58, 61, 72 n.6

União das Mulheres Socialistas (Union of Socialist Women), 118
Unions, 124
United States, 1, 70, 119, 121

Vasconcelos, Carolina Michaëlis de, 116
Vatican, 122
Veleda, Maria, 117
Velho da Costa, Maria, xiii, 1–23, 92 n.1
A Vida Sexual (The Sexual Life), 91

Vilamoura, 70
Virginity, 122–23
"Viúvas dos vivos" (widows of the
    living), 123. *See also* Emigration
"Voyage in," 22
The Voyage Out, 93–97
A Voz Feminina (Woman's Voice),
    114, 116

Wars in Africa, 6, 53, 55, 56, 69,
    72 n.4, 123. *See also* Africa
The Waves, 27
"Way of seeing," 8, 58
Witchcraft, 13
Woolf, Virginia, xiv, 1, 8–9, 23 n.3,
    27, 93–97
Wuthering Heights, 76
Women's: body, 4, 8, 10, 36, 42,
    110, 112; language, 10, 93–112;
    education, 114–16, 117, 119–20,

123, 126–27, 127 n.2; equality,
    115, 118, 120, 125, 128 n.3;
    espaços (spaces) 127; health
    care, 117, 127; legal rights, 2, 4,
    91, 113–29; liberation, 3, 7, 114;
    political organization, 114, 115,
    117–19, 121, 123–26, 127 n.3;
    political representation, 126;
    studies, 125; suffrage, 4, 114,
    115, 117–18, 120–21, 123; un-
    employment, 126; work, 2–3,
    115, 128 n.7
World War I, 55, 93, 119

Xerazade e os Outros, 25–48

Yeats, William Butler, 83

Zero: Romance Pré-Histórico (Zero:
    A Prehistoric Novel), 72 n.3